PERSUADED TO LIVE

PERSUADED TO LIVE

Conversion Stories from the
BILLY GRAHAM CRUSADES

BY ROBERT O. FERM

Including a Message by Billy Graham

INTRODUCTION BY FRANK E. GAEBELEIN

FLEMING H. REVELL COMPANY

Contents

Contents

Introduction

EVALUATIONS OF SUCH efforts as the Graham Crusades vary greatly. Some see their chief significance in the measure of Christian unity attained, others stress the evidence they give of Protestant vitality, while still others consider the Crusades a means of recruitment for the churches. These and similar outcomes of the ministry of Billy Graham and his associates are by no means irrelevant. Yet they do not in themselves express the chief purpose of the Crusades.

Surely the primary measure of the effectiveness of public evangelism is that of actual results in individual lives. Our Lord Himself gave us the criterion when He said, "By their fruits ye shall know them." All other considerations aside—and they are far from insignificant—the first question to be asked is always this: "What really happened to those who professed conversion?"

This book by a fair-minded observer goes far in answering that question. The author, Robert O. Ferm, has spent much time talking with men and women, not only in the United States but also abroad, who have been converted in the Graham meetings. Thus the stories contained in this book are not hearsay; they have all been verified at firsthand. They are told directly and simply, for in good part the converts speak for themselves. Although backgrounds and personalities differ widely, there is throughout the book a remarkable unanimity of witness to the transforming power of Christ experienced when men and women face their need, repent of their sins, and, by an act of the will, trust Him as Lord and Saviour.

A religious classic of former years is Harold Begbie's *Twice-Born Men*. And Dr. Ferm's modest but moving account of what happened to individuals through Billy Graham's forthright preaching of Christ is nothing less than another and present-day *Twice-Born Men*. Now that it is published, every honest appraisal of the Crusades must give due consideration to this book in which the indelible effect of the Gospel in human life is so vividly portrayed.

FRANK E. GAEBELEIN
Headmaster, Stony Brook School

Stony Brook, Long Island

1. *The Foolishness of Preaching*

"THREE MONTHS AFTER I made my decision for Christ, I tried going back to the old life, but I knew it would never satisfy me as it formerly did. I knew that God had changed me into a new person." This statement by one convert is the feeling of thousands who have been attracted first to a Billy Graham Crusade meeting and then to Christ.

What has happened to these persons? Thirty-eight thousand Londoners, fifty-two thousand Scotsmen, and over sixty thousand New Yorkers have been convinced they needed to commit their lives to Jesus Christ. They are but a part of an ever-growing host of converts. They had listened to the preaching of Billy Graham, although many of them admitted that they quite forgot the speaker after the first few minutes. Delinquents and professional people, college students and housewives, prostitutes and socialites all forgot their superficial differences as they listened together. It was an atmosphere they were unable to explain or understand. Something mysterious was taking place that they had never anticipated.

The Gospel transformed a skating arena into a church,

a public auditorium into a chapel and an amphitheater
into a cathedral. Whether indoors or out, the same impact
was felt again and again. A mass gathering became the
occasion when hundreds felt as if they were standing alone
before God to give an account of their lives. Slumbering
consciences were suddenly awakened to remind young
and old that all had sinned and come short of the glory
of God.

Although thousands gather for such Crusade meetings,
it is no mass psychology or movement. Every decision is
individual. Most of those who answered the invitation
have said "I felt as if I were alone." Psychologists and
psychiatrists have attempted to explain it, some unbelieving clerics have sought to discredit it, but there remains
an almost unbelievable number of practicing Christians
who will say "I found Jesus Christ in a Billy Graham
Crusade meeting."

Nearly everyone is interested in the convert. The em-
ployer will watch with considerable interest a secretary
who arrives at the office with a pleasant smile and cheerful
disposition. He will wonder what happened to the former
fearful and frustrated girl who now is radiant and happy.
He soon learns that she made a decision for Christ. Almost
immediately he confidently predicts, "It won't last." But as
days slip by and she remains buoyant and helpful, without
the former profanity or selfishness, he is all the more
amazed. He cannot explain it. Neither can the husband
explain why his nagging wife no longer oppresses him, nor
the wife explain why her philandering, drinking husband
has suddenly become considerate and cheerful.

Some of the converts from recent Crusades have had an

opportunity to tell their stories. In many respects they are like all converts, for no matter how different their former environment may have been, or how unlike their training and heredity, there came a moment when they vividly saw the great need of their lives. Past sins and wrongs could not be undone, and there were established habits that could not be broken. Eternity offered no possible hope for them. The horrible sense of being lost crept over them and there was nothing, absolutely nothing they could do for relief and comfort. That is, nothing they had ever tried until that moment.

Then in their distress and spiritual bankruptcy came a word of hope. It was a message that at first seemed to condemn. What was said seemed to pierce their very souls. It was as if a brilliant light had been turned on to reveal all the imperfections of the human heart. All the evil and violence was laid open to full view—nothing was hidden from the searchlight of the truth. All of their righteousness suddenly turned into filthy rags.

Was it a miracle? In that moment of unexpected searching of the heart, the solution was offered. To every one of them it seemed impossible, yet they were encouraged to hope and not be discouraged. They were not convinced because of clever arguments. They had not been swayed by eloquent speaking. It was the word of the cross they were hearing. If it had been heard before, it had sounded like foolishness, "For the preaching of the cross is to them that perish foolishness . . ." (I Corinthians 1:18). This time the message came with power. The magnetism of the cross seemed to lift them from their seats and carry them to the front and on to the counseling room.

What had these people heard? Many of them had tried
to be good. Some of them were beyond criticism; others
had been frequently found in some church in search of
spiritual uplift. But as both the good and bad listened,
a message penetrated the veneer of self-righteousness
and pretense. Billy Graham was preaching, and as he
preached there was an evident power and persuasiveness
that could not be accounted for by human reason. There
remained only one possible explanation. GOD. God was
honoring the preaching of the cross. The hearts of cal-
loused sinners were opened and a new life was begotten
as they listened.

One of the converts, as he thought of the experience,
said, "The longer you live in this world, the more you
realize there is a need for the foolishness of preaching.
In fact it isn't so foolish after all. This is a crazy world,
and now the Gospel makes sense for the first time. You
have to be saved to see it that way." He had sat in the
crowd many nights, listening to the songs and prayers.
Together with many others he had been sitting there
when Billy Graham came to the platform, and with an
urgent voice began:

A MESSAGE
BY BILLY GRAHAM[1]

"We have heard the voice of the philosopher, the
psychologist, the historian and the diplomat, as they try

[1] This sermon entitled "The Offense of the Cross" was delivered in
Madison Square Garden during the New York Crusade. It was printed in
the November 1957 issue of *Eternity* from whom permission has been
granted to include it here.

to solve the problems of the world, the nation, and our community. But have we yet heard what God has to say about them, and about you, your problems, your burdens, your difficulties, your perplexities?

"In Galatians 5:11, Paul speaks: 'And I, brethren, if I yet preach circumcision, why do I yet suffer persecution? then is the offense of the cross ceased.'

"That expression, 'offense of the cross,' at first may sound strange to the modern mind. For we have crosses on our churches, embossed on our Bibles, and as ornaments around our necks. The cross is an emblem of art to the poets. There may be nothing wrong with this sentimentality, but the Bible teaches that the cross as understood in New Testament days was an offense, a stumbling block, a scandal to men.

"Christ is not always attractive to the human heart, no matter how He is presented. Isaiah with prophetic vision says, as he looks down the corridors of time: 'There is no beauty in him that men should desire him.' Paul, living after Christ, found that the cross provoked the scorn and aroused the antagonism of men. When he held up Christ and Him crucified, many were offended and turned away in contempt and rage. Today we hear the cry all over the Christian world, 'Back to Christ.' I want to ask, 'What Christ are we to go back to?'

"I attended a conference at Princeton Seminary some time ago. The president of one of our theological seminaries remarked, 'I am convinced we are having a religious revival in America, but,' he said, 'it is not the Christian religion.' Sometimes when we look at Christ, we get a wrong concept of Him. Too often, He is only the Jesus who walked in Galilee, only the picture of wisdom in Jerusalem, or an ideal of a picturesque imagination. He is not the Christ of the cross. The cross in the days of Christ stood for a place of horrible execution. It was the place where murderers and the lowest criminals die—a place of horrible suffering, as well as terrible, tragic deaths. When Jesus said, 'If you are going to follow me, you have to take up a cross,' it was the same as saying, 'Come and bring your electric chair with you. Take up the gas chamber and follow me.' He did not have a beautiful gold cross in mind—the cross on a church steeple or on the front of your Bible. Jesus had in mind a place of execution.

"Paul found that wherever he went he had no difficulty until he began to preach the cross. Wherever he went he found that the cross was an offense, a stumbling block, a scandal. People did not want to talk about it, and they did not want to hear about it. After two thousand years it has not changed. In America, in Europe, in Asia, in Africa, the cross of our Lord Jesus Christ is still a stumbling block to men who want to go to Heaven but are not willing to pay the price of the cross.

"There are four reasons why the cross is an offense:

"Firstly, the cross of Christ condemns the world. The thief on the cross beside Christ, looked at Christ dying, confessed openly his sins, and said, 'Lord, remember me when thou comest into thy kingdom.' The fact that Christ was dying and His blood was being shed had thrown the searchlight on his own wickedness. He saw the purity, holiness, and righteousness of Christ, dying not for His own sins but for the sins of the whole world, and he recognized immediately that in comparison to Christ he was a sinner, and he cried out to God for salvation.

"That is how I know I am a sinner. Not only because I have broken the Ten Commandments, sin being a transgression of the law, but because I have come short of the glory of God. The glory of God is Christ, and, if I have failed to live like Jesus, to be as holy, good, pure, and righteous as Jesus was, I come short. I am a sinner. Who of you can stand up and say, 'I am as good as Jesus'? NONE of you can. For all have sinned and come short of the glory of God, and the wages of sin is death.

"Look at Herod. He was living in adultery—committing the sin that broke the Seventh Commandment. Now, you can commit adultery several ways. Jesus said that if you look upon a woman to lust after her, you have committed it already. A word, the dirty joke, obscene language, filthy literature that plays upon the imagination—it is the same as if you committed it. Herod condemned Christ because His purity, love and graciousness shone upon Herod's sins. Herod did not like it, and the cross became an offense to Herod. Neither do you like the cross. Either it will make you turn away and harden your heart, or it will melt your heart and bring you to the foot of the cross, where Jesus will forgive you, cleanse and make you pure.

"Caiaphas, filled with pride, and cold, crafty wisdom, faced Christ, and the shadow of the cross pointed as a dagger at Caiaphas. He saw his own selfishness, but he

could not stand it, and the cross became an offense to him
—and to all of you filled with your ego and pride.

"The sin of Pilate was fear. He was a moral coward.
How many people would give their life to Christ, but
they are afraid of what the crowd or the neighbors will
say. They are afraid to face their family. So, as to Pilate,
the cross becomes a stumbling block.

"The cross shone in the direction of Judas, filled with
covetousness, greed, and ambition. He wilted and became
a suicide, because the cross was a stumbling block. Judas
could follow Christ when the people were cheering: Judas
was right there in the parade on Palm Sunday when
the band was playing and everything was going fine. But,
when the chips were down, and Jesus began to talk about
a cross, Judas said, 'Count me out.' He was putting his
money and his ambition above God. Has money come
between you and God? A few weeks ago a man accepted
Jesus Christ and said, 'From now on, although my business
may go broke, I shall make only honest dollars.' It may
cost you that to give your life to Christ.

"Look at the Apostle Paul. Wherever he went to preach,
the cross was an offense. He preached before Felix, and
the burning message of the cross condemned Felix so
that he trembled, but he said, 'When I have a more convenient season I'll call for you, Paul. Go away.' There
never came a more convenient season for Felix. That was
his last hour and he did not know it. A man in the gallery
one night during the Crusade trembled. He gripped the
seat until his fingers throbbed with blood. He went home
and dropped dead that night. Paul preached the cross to

Festus who cried out, 'Paul you are mad; you are a raving maniac.' The cross is an offense. Agrippa, the great king, was so moved when Paul preached the cross to him that he said, 'Almost, thou persuadest me to become a Christian.' Agrippa was close to the Kingdom, but he missed it as though he had missed it by ten million miles. He was willing to believe in Jesus, to believe in God, to believe in the church. He was willing to believe in some of the ethical concepts of Christianity. He was *not* willing to come to the cross, acknowledge he was a sinner, renounce his sins, and receive the Saviour. The Scripture says, 'Men love darkness because their deeds are evil.' The cross throws spiritual light into the dark recesses of our souls and shows us our sins. The cross becomes an offense because it condemns us as sinners.

"Secondly, the cross is an offense because blood was shed there. People say this is a slaughter-house religion, a repulsive religion of blood. From Genesis to Malachi in the Old Testament you will read of blood and blood being shed. All through the New Testament you will read of the blood of Christ. It is repulsive to some, but God put it there, and it means this: Blood means life. 'The life of the flesh is in the blood.' When blood is shed, life goes. Jesus gave His life on the cross when He shed His life's blood. It is the blood of propitiation—Romans 3:25: 'Whom God hath set forth to be a propitiation through faith in his blood, to declare his righteousness for the remission of sins that are past. . . . ' It is the blood of redemption—Revelation 5:9: 'And they sung a new song, saying, Thou art worthy to take the book, and to open the seals thereof; for thou wast slain, and hast redeemed us to God by thy blood out of every kindred, and tongue, and people, and nation. . . . ' It is the blood of remission or forgiveness—Hebrews 9:22: 'And almost all things are by the law purged with blood; and without shedding of blood is no remission.' If Christ had not shed His blood on the cross, we could never be forgiven of our sins. It is the blood of reconciliation—Ephesians 2:13: 'But now in Christ Jesus ye who sometimes were far off are made nigh by the blood of Christ.' We were separated from God by sins, but the blood of Christ brought us back to God again. That is why many of you are in agony. You make money, but you are not satisfied. You have glamour, you go to amusements, you drink alcohol, but you do not have satisfaction in yourself. Your soul was made in the image of God, but your sins and iniquities have separated between you and your God. There is only one way to find peace and forgiveness, and that is by the cross.

"It is the blood of justification—justified by His blood, we shall be saved from wrath through Him, says the Bible. It is the blood of peace. Peace is found at the cross and only at the cross. It is the blood of entrance into His presence: 'Having therefore, brethren, boldness to enter into the holiest by the blood of Jesus . . .' (Hebrews 10:19). Because Christ died and shed His blood on that cross, I have a right in the name of Christ to come into the very presence of God. It is the blood of Christ: 'But if we walk in the light, as he is in the light, we have fellowship one with another, and the blood of Jesus Christ his Son cleanseth us from all sin' (I John 1:7).

"It is said the devil once confronted Martin Luther with a tabulation of his sins. Luther asked, 'Is that all?' 'No!' said the devil, 'There are many more.' Martin Luther said, 'Put them down.' The devil sneeringly wrote them down, and Martin Luther said, 'Is that all you can think of?' The devil said, 'Yes. Now what?' 'Now,' said Martin Luther, 'write beneath them all, "The blood of Jesus Christ cleanseth from all sin."' There is a fountain filled with blood, drawn from Immanuel's veins and sinners plunged beneath that flood lose all their guilty stains. In the will of J. P. Morgan, the great financier of Wall Street, many dispositions were made, some of large sums of money that affected the financial equilibrium of the world, but here is what he said to his children in his will. 'I commit my soul into the hands of my Saviour, full of confidence that having redeemed me and washed me with His most precious blood, He will present me faultless before the throne of my heavenly Father. I entreat my children to maintain and defend at all hazards, and at any cost of personal sacrifice, the blessed doctrine of complete atonement of sin through the blood of Jesus Christ, once offered, and through that alone.' J. P. Morgan was just as dependent on the cross of Christ as the dying thief. I tell you when I come to the entrance of the Kingdom of Heaven I am not going to say, 'Well, I preached to a large crowd of people at Madison Square Garden.' I am not going to plead, 'Lord, I have tried to live a good life.' I am not going to boast, 'But, Lord, I wrote out a check and gave my money to You.' None of that. I am going to plead the cross of Christ. There is no other hope.

"Thirdly, the cross of Christ is an offense because it sets forth an imperative ideal of life. Jesus said, 'If any man will come after me, let him deny himself, and take up his cross, and follow me.' We are busy in our churches today building astronomical figures—sending in reports. How many new members we took in. How many people affiliated with the church. Jesus worked on the opposite end. Every time the crowd got too big, Jesus would say, 'All right, deny yourself if you want to follow me.' That eliminated about half of them. To those remaining He would say, 'All right, if you are going to follow me, take up the cross.' That eliminated almost all the rest of them. They did not want self-denial; they wanted a kingdom, they wanted a crown, they wanted to rule, to live in a palace. They wanted all the blessings of the Christian life, but they were not going to go to the cross with Him. How many chafe at the restraint of a life like Christ's! We refuse to give up what we know His cross condemns. In a great city like New York, with its sensual indulgences of rich and poor, with its neglect of the miserable in the slum areas and the careless eye toward the wretched condition of thousands, with the selfish attitudes in the growing race problem, we see the evidence that the cross is an offense to us. Oh, how many times Christians get disturbed about this. I imagine the rich man passing by Lazarus got disturbed when he saw Lazarus lying there. Yet the rich man went to hell because of his neglect of the poor man. It does not say that he hated Lazarus; he did not kick him in the teeth, put him in prison, or do anything against him. Undoubtedly he believed in God, but he neglected the poor man.

"The offense of the cross. Cross-bearing means that I go back to my community and witness for Christ, that I go back to my home and live for Christ. A Christ-directed, Christ-controlled life means that I become the right kind of a husband, and father, or wife, and mother.

"We were holding one of our first Crusades in Georgia in 1947. It was about 2:00 o'clock in the morning and in a big room next door to us in the hotel they were having the wildest party I think I have ever heard or seen. They were tearing the roof down—singing lewd songs, swearing, drinking, all of which we could hear. It was impossible to sleep. Grady Wilson came to my room and asked, 'What shall we do?' I put on my bathrobe, went next door and knocked. A man answered and asked, 'What do you want?' 'Well,' I said, 'I am a minister, and tomorrow, or today, is Sunday. We are trying to get some sleep next door, but we can't.' He turned to the crowd packed in there. 'Say, wait a minute everybody. Here is a preacher who says he wants to talk to us.' Boy, I gave it to them, and they all listened. I said, 'I bet most of you are church members, and some of you are Sunday school teachers even.' One lady with tears streaming down her cheeks said, 'Mr. Graham, you're right, I am a Sunday school teacher.' The offense of the cross. How do you act when no other Christians are around? Do you live for Christ, witness for Christ? Do you let them know where you stand?

"Lastly, the cross of Christ is an offense because it claims to be the power and salvation of God. It demands from every man as his first duty that he get right with God. We do not like that. We like to think that there are other roads to heaven beside the one road. Jesus said that the gate to heaven is narrow. At the beginning of that gate is a cross, and no man will ever gain entrance to the Kingdom of Heaven unless he comes by way of the cross. The cross humbles us, the cross demands, the cross expects everything we have to be given to Christ. The cross condemns every other way of salvation. Man and his ego says, 'I am going my own way.' Many are sincere. They think they are going to make it, but if there were any other way to salvation, Christ would never have gone to the cross. He would never have died. He prayed in the Garden of Gethsemane, 'If thou be willing, remove this cup from me: nevertheless not my will, but thine, be done.'

"I tell you as a minister of the Gospel of Christ that there is *no other way* one can be saved but this. Have you been saved? Have you trusted in Christ? You can find a new life here and now and eternal life to come, because you become a partaker of God's life the moment you come to the cross. Jesus finished the work. You don't have to add to it. All you do is receive it."

2. A Reporter Hears the Good News

BILL HAD JUST COME from the desk of the chief editor with
his assignment for the next six weeks. He was to cover
the nightly meetings held at the Madison Square Garden
in New York. It was the Billy Graham Crusade, and was
considered to be possible front-page news for a few nights
at least. For Bill it was routine, for he was religious reporter for the press association.

He wasn't even excited as he hurried along Eighth
Avenue and found his seat in the press section. He was
used to religious rallies and conventions. He had reported
some of the largest ever held in New York. Now he was
seated directly in front of the giant platform where he
could get an excellent look at the world-famed evangelist.
His mind was already made up, and he thought he could
write up the meeting in advance, having read much about
the evangelist and the earlier Crusades. He was a seasoned
reporter and knew all the technique of telling a story. As
a reporter he must be objective, always the observer but
never participating in what takes place.

Long before the meetings began, they were viewed as
good news. What Bill didn't know was that he would be

hearing the best news of all. Members of the Billy Graham
team and guests seated on the platform observed the reporters with great interest. They experienced a special
thrill from time to time as members of the press would forget their occupation as reporters and leave the press section to join the inquirers that seek the Lord. Each time this
happened, Bill would be shocked and disturbed. Although
he had been reporting every manner of religious activity in
the metropolitan area, this meeting was different. Something was happening to people. There was a conviction
that few could resist.

At first it seemed that the preacher was just giving the
people what they wanted, but when he invoked the demands of the law, even saints were compelled to examine
themselves, and sinners were left without any defense. But
the evangelist never stopped when his audience had been
awakened to a sense of personal sin and guilt. He went on
to make plain the divinely appointed way by which sinful
man and a Holy God could be reconciled. From the first
night there was a sense of the presence of God in the very
same auditorium where only three days before the circus
elephants had performed to amuse a crowd that never
quite filled the balconies. This sense of the presence of
God was an intangible something that a reporter could
not put into words. Bill was having difficulty.

He wrote about an unprecedented crowd, and the over-
flow that jammed 49th Street. He described the left-over
smell of the circus animals and bunting that was draped
about. He told of the mammoth platform decorated with
live plants and evergreen. Even the hundreds of other

reporters and cameras he remembered to make note of. But when all of that had been written, he found his greatest task remaining. He could not account for the hundreds who left their seats and came from the farthest balcony to stand in the open area in front of the platform to declare publicly their desire to receive forgiveness and eternal life.

Neither could Bill describe the strange thing that was happening to his own way of thinking and reporting. He had heard this kind of Bible preaching as a boy somewhere in the pan-handle of Oklahoma. As one who was well informed in history, he had never doubted the historical facts that are uniquely Christian. He knew that Christ had been on earth and had been unjustly tried and executed as a criminal. He knew that the grave had failed to hold its victim, but that Jesus had triumphed over death by His resurrection. Now these historical facts were being applied to his own conscience, and he was becoming uncomfortable, especially when he kept trying to remember that he was there to report, and not to be converted.

In his vivid way, Bill told of the experience. "I went to report several nights before I got the full voltage." Speaking in the age long before the discovery of electricity, Jesus had said, "The wind bloweth where it listeth, and thou hearest the sound thereof, but canst not tell whence it cometh, and whither it goeth: so is every one that is born of the Spirit." Bill was feeling the wind of the Spirit but was not able to define it in the brilliant language of a writer. Now he was hearing what he always had known, but it was bearing in upon him with a power he had never felt before.

"Somehow I had gotten away from it in my more mature years. My wife and I differ in our views on religion. We used to get into some hot arguments over it. She had gone to a college where the Bible is not accepted, and where skepticism is the fashion. I used to tell her she was still a college girl or she wouldn't be the skeptic she was. As for me, I had always believed, in theory. My assignments occasionally called for Bible study, and not long ago I published a book on the people who knew Jesus."

There is a vast difference between knowing Jesus as a character in history and knowing Him as the Saviour. Bill had this to learn after his book was complete. Those who express their views on religion and religious conversion cannot always detect this difference.

Bill continued to tell his story. "A newsman must be on the sidelines. I sat there with many fellow reporters. One night when I felt the compulsion of the call it was as if some superhuman power had hold of me. I didn't go, for there was a conflict with my responsibility as a reporter. I must not get involved in the movement lest I cease being a reporter. To a reporter, God doesn't mean a thing. To me now He means everything. It's all so strange, because I really went to see how effective Billy actually was. My executive editor had told me about him, but I wanted to go for myself.

"Night after night I sat there. After the one time when I felt that compulsion to go, it became a real conflict. I remember telling the boss one time that if I kept on going I'd soon become a convert myself. He warned me of becoming involved and even threatened to fire me if I ever did so. I suppose I was a coward because night after night I sat there all the time knowing I should join those who were answering the invitation. Then one night something very wonderful and different happened.

"After the meeting was over on a certain night I did what any reporter would do. I was going after a story. I wanted something that contained the human interest angle. So I started down Eighth Avenue to visit bar-keepers. I thought that here would be an angle which I hadn't tried yet. I made my way from bar to bar, in each case getting the same story of bad business. Again and again I would hear how this crowd wasn't a drinking crowd. In fact, one of the bars just across the street finally closed for the summer.

"As I emerged from the last bar I had planned to visit that night, I met a young girl who worked at the Crusade office. She greeted me very pleasantly. We chatted a moment, and I told her about my excursions that night. I invited her to join me for a cup of coffee and a snack. As we sat there talking, she asked what my findings were. We talked all about those who were finding their peace with God, and then she asked me about my own soul. I told her what a coward I was. I told her how I had often felt drawn to answer the call but that I was a reporter. I told her of my fear of what my friends would say. I even confessed that I knew I should have received Christ that night.

"Then Margaret began to talk to me. I was at first amazed at her courage. I was a college man and she had never been to college. I was a top-rank reporter and she was a secretary. I had employed secretaries who were frightened to express their views to me, but she began to speak to me with an authority that reminded me of Billy. She just kept thumbing through her Bible and giving me Scripture. What she gave me was what I had thought were just trite phrases and clichés, but somehow that night they were different. Then she insisted that I pray. I recoiled at the idea of praying there in a coffee shop.

"Then suddenly my head dropped to the table. I felt flushed and somewhat embarrassed, but my sense of the presence of God was overwhelming. I prayed. Right then, in the public of a coffee shop, Jesus Christ became personal to me and I knew the change had come. Now all that had been theory for so many years became a reality. Jesus Christ had suddenly stepped out of the first century into the twentieth so far as I was concerned.

"I went home that night a new person. It's a change that a reporter can't write up exactly, and if he does, the unconverted person can't grasp it anyhow. You just have to have it happen to you. When I got home, my wife told me that she had gone forward that night! She had never before gotten beyond intellectual skepticism. I had been the defender of Christianity. But both of us had needed Christ.

"My wife had gone to the Garden at my request. I had been so impressed by Billy's preaching that I had wanted her to hear him. I had thought the sermon wasn't as good as the night before, and it was a surprise to me that she was so impressed. Now I know that a sermon isn't always to be judged on the basis of its literary excellence but on the basis of its effects on our lives. After my wife had heard him and the invitation was given, she responded at once. She certainly didn't go because she thought it was the thing to do. In fact she was naturally opposed to such demonstration. After the experience was over, she told me that when she went down the aisle, she felt inside like a Bendix washer! Today she is a radiant Christian.

"But to finish my own story, I returned to the Garden the next night to report again. The big difference was that I had made up my mind to join the inquirers just to take my stand before my fellow reporters. I wanted my decision to be made public." After the night of his decision in the coffee shop, Bill had done some close thinking about what had happened. He had placed himself at the head of the list of all the people in New York he never expected to go forward. As he talked and thought about his experience that had meant so much to him, he said, "The longer you live in this world, the more you realize there is a need for the 'foolishness' of preaching. In fact, it isn't so foolish after all. This is a crazy world, and now the Gospel makes sense for the first time. You have to be saved to see it that way."

Some would say that it was not surprising that Bill should make the decision, because of his childhood training. This would never explain the conversion of those who make their decision the first night they ever hear the Gospel.

Bill told of the days that had passed since he and his wife had made their decision. For one thing, he said that their home was a changed place. There had been a time

when religion couldn't be discussed in the home without
bitterness. Now they are radiant Christians, and their conversation in the home concerns the great things that God
had done for them.

He also told of a new attitude toward his work. As a
reporter he must remain aloof and report what is happening. But now he can report what happens when a soul is
born again, for he knows what takes place. His conversion is another example of those remarkable events in the
lives of persons of all sorts. This reminds us again of the
words of the Saviour when He said, "The wind bloweth
where it listeth, and thou hearest the sound thereof, but
canst not tell whence it cometh, and whither it goeth: so
is every one that is born of the Spirit."

3. Out of the Depths

AMERICAN SOCIETY is haunted with the fact that more than
fifty thousand persons a year are becoming alcoholics.
Most of the crimes committed are committed while people are under the influence of alcohol and the majority of
auto accidents can be attributed to its use. In the city of

New York, where personal identity becomes lost in the vast crowd, alcoholism is a major problem. The Bowery has been known around the world for many years as the street of forgotten men. But there are thousands of unknown persons who are alcoholic or are becoming so every day.

Many and varied attempts have been made to cure the alcoholic, but no cure of alcoholism is as startling as the new birth. To this remarkable deliverance many gave witness. Some of them have been interviewed and their stories recorded in order that others, who had lost hope of deliverance, might dare to believe that there is a way. One of them, Jane, wrote her testimony, and was later interviewed. Her deliverance from alcohol and from the power of sin in her life is one of the trophies of the Crusade.

"My father was alcoholic, so I have lived with it all my life. When I was twelve, my parents were divorced, and mother remarried. I always felt as though I were in the way. I didn't blame her for separating from father, because I can still remember him almost killing her when he would come home drunk. It was a hell on earth.

"I went to work at seventeen for a wealthy family. The man taught me to drink, and I began to drink regularly. Before long they moved away and I went home again. I couldn't stay there, and took domestic work again to try to earn my way through high school. It was too much for me, and I got to drinking more than ever. Drinking has ruined everything in my life. I didn't want to be what I was, but I couldn't leave it alone once I started. All my life when it seemed I had something, it would blow up.

Once I started going to church, but I had to move. I didn't
start going again in the new area. When I went out it was
usually with older girls, and they always drank.

"After my sister got married she had an illegitimate
child. In an attempt to drown her sorrow and mine, we
spent the next year drinking heavily. At that time I
thought of God and wondered why He should help me.
I was too far gone. Soon I met and married a fellow who
was worse than I was. He wouldn't work, but he made me
work. He was drunk all the time so after three years I
divorced him. My second marriage was not much better.
This time I played a dirty trick on the guy and he started
drinking. After three years we broke up. Then I joined the
army and for a time I was an ambulance driver. I had a
love affair that I thought was just right during that time,
but it didn't last. I always was looking for the ideal. While
in the army I would go to church once in a while, but I
never did know a thing about the Bible. I was totally
ignorant of Christ and salvation.

"After a third unsuccessful marriage, I finally was married a fourth time to an Asian. We opened a restaurant,
but the grind of a seventeen-hour day drove me to drink
again. I suppose you think I couldn't face hard life. I
know I shouldn't have turned to liquor every time I hit a
tough situation, but in my weakness I couldn't think of
any other way of escape. I can't tell you how much I
drank, nor how much I wished I could get away from it.
I just didn't have the power in myself. I finally sank to the
depths with drink. I can still remember one day as I sat in
a little room off the restaurant, I was in despair. I had not

an ounce of will of my own. I wanted to die, but that day was a turning point. I think God helped me get sober long enough to hear the Gospel.

"We sold the restaurant that day, and then a night or two later, I went to Madison Square Garden. I'll never forget that night, because it was the most wonderful night of my life. I listened to Billy Graham, and as he preached, I knew God was speaking through him and I knew the message was for me. I remember he told how there was no one, no matter how far down that person might have gone, whom God wouldn't save for Jesus' sake. He described the suffering of Christ very vividly and then he said, 'Did you know that Christ did all that for you that He might save you from all your sins?'

"I had heard about Jesus a time or two, and seemed to recall someone telling that He had died on a cross. But all that didn't seem to have anything to do with my poor miserable life. I couldn't imagine that God would be interested in me after the terible things I had done. It was all so horrible. I think that God must have even helped me to believe, because I was too far gone even for that.

"That night, I was glad to go forward when Billy asked all of us to come to receive Christ. I felt that it was all too good to be true. I didn't dare to believe that this could be the end of a horrible past and the beginning of a wonderful new life. But that is just what happened. God took me up that night and saved my poor soul.

"It was several days before I could make sense out of it. In fact, I didn't go back to the meeting the next night. After just a few days it all did begin to make sense. I

knew that God had changed my life because He took fear
out of my life. Alcoholics are always afraid, but I'm not
afraid any more. Most of them don't want to go on drinking because it's a living hell, but they have lost all their
strength and can't help themselves.

"I began to read the Bible. It was an entirely new thing
for me, because I had no knowledge of it at all. I also received a copy of Billy Graham's book, *Peace with God*,
and that has been a wonderful help to me. I enrolled in
one of the Bible classes and have even joined a church.
I never knew life could be so wonderful. I have never
known anything like this since I was born."

Another woman who had lived a miserable life because
of drinking was Sarah. She and her two small children
were visited in their home in a basement apartment. Only
one small window in the front and another in the rear of
the apartment provided light and ventilation. Poverty and
sordidness were evident, but things were happening. The
new-found faith had given a new motivation and drive
that before had been lacking.

The children appeared to be from separate families, and
Sarah explained that the older was from a former marriage
and the younger belonged to her present husband. Another child had died when they first arrived in New York.

She said that her mother had been a church member.
Her father had no religion.

"In spite of such a divided home," she recalled, "I did
have some religious training. I always believed that Jesus

had come into the world and died, but it was certainly never meaningful to me. I lived as if He never had come at all. I must admit that I was always troubled, and once in a while would go to church to see if I might get help. I don't need to tell you I never did. Even my baptism and confirmation confused me. I never did know why you did such things.

"In 1946 I was married to a man who was an alcoholic. With him I lived a miserable life. He spent all we had on liquor and we lived on almost no money. I drank some. There wasn't enough money for both of us to drink heavily. Shortly after we came to New York he died. He left me with this child," she said, as she pointed to a girl of five, "and I didn't know what to do then. I didn't have enough money to move back to Ohio. I got odd jobs to keep going. It was then that I began drinking heavily. I met my present husband in a tavern one night, and we started going together. After a while we were married. I must say that he isn't an alcoholic. He does drink now and then. I was the one who became addicted.

"I can't blame anyone now for my miserable condition. My husband has had steady work, but we, I should say I, have just wasted everything—drank all our money up until we couldn't seem to get out of this mess. It was on a Saturday night when we were watching television that I first heard Billy Graham. I thank God that they had that program on TV or I might not ever have heard anything about it. I was glued to the TV set for that hour, and after it was over I just couldn't look at another program that night. It seemed too sacred. God had spoken to me.

"I decided to go and hear Billy in person, so the next free night I had, I went. You can't believe the change that took place. I can't remember any particular Scripture Billy quoted, but he did make the Way to Jesus clear. He said there was hope for the most wicked. He preached on a woman taken in adultery. All of a sudden, I received hope and was encouraged to leave my seat and go down to the front to be born again.

"It all happened just like he said. He said that a person could go out completely changed. I did.

"I'll never forget that night. As I went forward, I wept. I couldn't control my weeping. I had been such an awful sinner, and to think that Christ could save me from it all was almost more than I could understand, but the Lord helped me to understand it. The lady who prayed for me gave me a little book on John. I hadn't read or seen a Bible for such a long time. That was all I had for a while. I have a Bible now." She held up a ragged Bible that had been cast off by someone, but to Sarah it was very precious. It was the Word of God, and her soul was finding nourishment through it.

"When I got home, my husband noticed a difference. He had seen me come in drunk so many times, but this time I came in singing, 'This is my story, this is my song.' He is Greek, and although he hardly ever goes to his church, he wasn't happy over my decision. After a few weeks he was glad though, because I wasn't drinking any more, and I was much easier to get along with. He is glad because of the change in me. He hasn't made a decision yet, but he is going to church with me once in a while."

Sarah still has her problems. There is still the problem of poverty and a dingy apartment, but she has found new strength with which to endure them. Her great victory has been over liquor. She hasn't had a drink since the night she claimed the Saviour. God delivered her from both the guilt and power of sin in one tremendous work of His grace.

Drunkenness leaves behind a train of problems and remorse. Violet found that what might have been a wonderful life had been ruined by her uncontrollable appetite for alcohol. Although she was a beautiful girl of thirty, the evidences of dissipation and a hard life were apparent. She tried to remember her early years at home, but all she could remember was that then she had had a good home and good parents, but that there was no religious influence at all. It is one of the American tragedies that so many persons are able to live in this country and remain totally ignorant of the Gospel. None of her friends were ever interested in church, and she said, "I just didn't know what a Christian was."

Violet's father was a traveling man. He didn't drink heavily but she recalled that there was always liquor in the house.

"When I was sixteen," Violet said, "my mother died, and I dropped out of school to take care of my father and a brother. I kept the home together for some time. One evening at dinner, father suggested that whiskey was very good in coffee. He gave me some, and from the first drink

I had a craving for more. I knew where he kept his liquor, and I would often drink so much that he would come home to find me passed out on the floor. What I cannot understand is that neither my father nor my brother were very disgusted. They would just put me to bed until I was sober again.

"After several years of this, I met and married a real nice guy whom I had known in school. He was a wonderful person, and I loved him dearly. But I couldn't control my appetite for liquor. I felt I must have it or die. I used to run out on him and go to a bar and sit there until I was too drunk to get home. I finally asked him for a divorce, and gave him grounds for it. All I wanted was someone to drink with.

"One night while I was sitting in the bar getting drunk, a young sailor came in and sat with me. We began to talk, and we soon decided to get married. I never did love him, and married him just so I'd have someone to drink with. I should have known that no marriage would be successful on such a basis. No sooner had we gotten married, than he was off on his own to drink. He made me stay home. He told so many lies about me that I didn't dare look my neighbors in the face. We had two lovely boys, and I thought surely this would settle him down. But he wanted to have all the privileges of being married without any of the responsibility.

"I was like a prisoner, locked up in my home for five years. He spent all our money on liquor. We didn't have more than a box to sit on and rags for clothing. Then we found a job as superintendents of an apartment house. Everything went well for a while until he demanded that

I give him the rent money we had collected from the other tenants. I had to give it to him or he would beat me black and blue, as he so often did.

"On a Saturday night when I was home, I sat drinking in front of television, when Billy Graham began to preach. I listened. I knew the Spirit of God was speaking to me. I had never heard the Gospel until that night. I felt so unclean as I listened. I knew that I would have to go to the meeting and hear more. I managed to get a neighbor to watch my boys for me and I went. I found a seat way in the back of the building. I was self-conscious because of having two blackened eyes and being all bruised from beatings my husband had given me.

"I listened to Billy Graham preach, and realized how much I needed God. He told how a person could be born again. I didn't know what it meant, but I thought it meant to start over. I certainly wanted to start over. So when people started going forward, I felt I must go. I was counseled by a real nice woman, but was so aware of my terrible appearance that I didn't hear what she said. I couldn't stop crying. It was real repentance for me. I knew that I was far from God. But she did tell me that God loved me and proved it by sending Jesus to die for me. It was almost too much to believe, especially for me.

"When I went home, I went to sleep for the first time in many weeks. I felt so relieved. I knew God had forgiven me. I can't explain how wonderful it was to know that the past could be forgiven. One good thing was, my husband didn't come in that night. He had been staying out night after night gambling.

"The next day was the day when the owner of the building came to get money we had collected for rent from the tenants, and I was supposed to lie for my husband. He had taken the money and beaten me without mercy when I told him it was wrong. When the owner came, I couldn't lie to him. Before my conversion it would have been easy, but now that God had saved me, I couldn't do it. I told him what had happened, and that I didn't have the money. He immediately reported it to the police. When my husband came home, I was afraid he would beat me worse than ever for telling. But the police had been waiting for him, and they grabbed him before he got into the house. Then they made me put the boys in a home until I could properly care for them. I was so proud of them. They were beautiful boys, but I had no way to support them. They were hungry most of the time and never well clothed.

"I had been so much a prisoner to liquor and my husband for the last five years I didn't know what to go. This was the beginning of a new kind of life for me. I got a job as a teleprinter, and am doing very well in my new work. Not long after all this had happened, I met my former husband one day. At first I was ashamed even to look at him. He was very kind to me, and so was his wife. He saw how much I was in need and offered help, but I was too proud. I told him I could get along. I learned from a friend that he is a very prosperous contractor on Long Island. I left him because I thought his way of life was boring, and chose the hell I have had instead.

"Now I know that all this had happened to me because

I gave in to the sinful drives that controlled me, as a result of not knowing Jesus and not having Him as my Saviour and Lord. I still feel very weak, but such a change has taken place that I could never go back to the old life again. God has opened up a new world for me.

"Now I'm working to get my boys back with me. I don't know how I can do it, but it's the one thing I want. I don't know if I ever will have a home and family life. I guess I threw that away when I left my first husband. But if I don't, I know the Lord will give me strength to go on and serve Him."

There were men and women who came to the Crusade meetings night after night with all the marks of dissipation and overindulgence. They slipped in with the crowd as if they were ashamed of their dirty, ragged clothing that fitted them poorly because it had been made for someone else. They were often slightly under the influence of some drug or alcohol, and occasionally one would actually stagger in to a seat somewhere in the Garden. No one knew what brought them in, and apart from the hidden working of the Holy Spirit, there would be no explanation. There was the seaman who came in one night. He had been a "dope pusher," and for want of a place to go, and being attracted by the lighted sign, came to the meeting. As he spoke to the counselor, he was advised to avoid the old crowd until he could gain a victory over dope. But he smiled, saying, "I'm not afraid to go and tell them what God did for me tonight."

After more than six weeks had passed, he returned from a transoceanic trip and visited the Garden again. He sought out the young man who counseled him the night he came to Christ and told him, "I'm still enjoying the blessing of salvation I received six weeks ago. I haven't had any dope since, and I never want it again. I'm going straight for the rest of my life with God's help."

Having a knowledge of the Gospel and being surrounded with Christian friends does not make a Christian. From the many recorded experiences of those who met Christ during the Crusade, it is clear that it is a supernatural change that can never be accounted for on the basis of a natural explanation. Those who sought to give a natural explanation for the power that was present in the meetings were completely baffled. A psychiatrist sat through five meetings in his attempt to analyze it. Then God analyzed him. He too joined the thousands who had begun to live by taking Christ as their Lord and Saviour.

The reporter who came nightly to report the Crusade was himself to come under God's influence and power. More than one skeptic who came to criticize was transformed, and not a few church members discovered that what they had always thought was Christianity was nothing more than a Christian ethic and veneer.

One of the latter group was Frank who came to one of the first meetings of the Crusade. He had known a Christian influence at home, though there was no systematic Bible reading or teaching there. His parents were immigrants from Norway and had raised a family in the slums of Brooklyn. Frank had fine taste and loved music, which he had studied until he was nineteen. But there was no money available to help him continue a musical career. He tried dentistry, but this too had to be given up for financial reasons. Going from one job to another became a discouraging ordeal.

Finally, as an insurance reporter, Frank got into the high-salary bracket. His occasional visit to church and his periodic participation in church life seemed to make only a slight impression on him. His reasons for attending church varied from being on the basketball team to listening to a nephew play the organ. Never did he find spiritual satisfaction. On one occasion he remembered a Sunday school teacher who had helped him a little, but never did anyone seek to direct him to the full assurance of faith in Christ.

"I went from a nominal religion to a very bad life," he recalled. "I began to drink heavily, and on account of much drinking I lost many good jobs. I frequently borrowed money from friends, but never tried to repay them. I spent it all on drink. I became very profane. It was so bad that I lost two jobs just because of my swearing. Many men swear, but mine was so bad that even the average man was offended. I couldn't talk without it. I didn't know how to express myself without profanity.

"After more than ten years of such a life, I was again drawn to the church. My nephew became organist, and I was very proud of him. It was what I had always wanted to do, but hadn't had the chance. In this church the min-

ister was very helpful. He held my interest and kept me
coming. Some time before the Crusade, the pastor announced a prayer meeting for the Crusade. He asked me
to come and I did. The people prayed for the meeting, but
I couldn't pray. I just listened. I became troubled the
more I thought about it. When the Crusade finally did
start, I couldn't go. By the time the meeting was held at
Forest Hills, I was so troubled I couldn't stay away. I'll
never forget it. I got in a taxi and before I knew it I was
telling the taxi driver about my concern. He turned to me
and said 'God bless you, sir, I'll be praying for you as you
listen to Mr. Graham.' That shocked me, for I didn't expect
a New York cab driver to be concerned about my problem.

"I didn't make a decision that day. It was nearly a week
later when I finally accepted Christ as my Saviour. That
night I knew something was going to happen. I got to the
Garden when it was almost full, and ran up to the second
balcony. As I ran, I could hear them singing 'Blessed assurance, Jesus is mine,' and I wished so much that I had
this assurance. I had heard some of Billy Graham's sermons on the Ten Commandments. This night he preached
on Jonah and his preaching to Nineveh. The sermon was
about repentance, and I knew then that being a Christian
was more than just believing that certain things were true.
You had to repent of your sins and confess them to God.

"I made my decision that night. I knew I would have to,
because it seemed that I would never have such a chance
again. As Billy kept giving Bible verses in his sermon, they
went into my heart like arrows. I could almost feel them
strike. Every time my sin would come up in front of me,

and I felt lost. But Billy never finished a sermon without telling about the hope that God gave us. This night as he told about the hope, I felt I must go forward and accept Christ. I kept thinking about the verse that says, 'For God so loved the world, that he gave his only begotten Son, that whosoever believeth in him should not perish, but have everlasting life.'

"I was relieved when I had finally made the step. I knew God had forgiven me for Jesus' sake. I knew that he had cleansed me from all my sins, according to the Bible. I wanted to do something right away. I asked if I could join the choir, and for the next ninety-three nights I sang to the glory of God every night. That was when the real joy came into my life.

"I went back to my job the day after I took the Saviour and told them all about it. The men just listened as if they couldn't believe it. They thought I must be crazy. They are nearly all of another faith, and though they had not been to hear Billy Graham, they were very interested in what had happened. The very first thing they noticed was that I didn't swear any more. God had taken all that away from me. I didn't do a thing about it. I have heard of some having a struggle, but I didn't. I don't believe I ever swore after that night. That is what the men themselves said about me. Of course I am through with drinking and all my dirty habits.

"A very wonderful thing has happened in our church. Before the Crusade, a group began to pray for God's blessing. We never knew how He would answer that

prayer. Now there are many in our church who have put
their trust in Jesus and have been saved.

"When the Crusade closed, some of us thought that the
prayer meetings would cease too. The prayer meetings are
still going strong. We have more things to pray about now
than ever. We pray for the pastor, and the church; we
pray for unconverted people who have been in the church
for years. We pray for Billy Graham and already are praying for the San Francisco Crusade.

"I can never tell you how much it has meant to me. I
can see the meaning of church and enjoy its services. Our
pastor is teaching the Bible to us now. Everything seems
different now that Christ has come into my life and taken
over."

4. *They Thought It Was a Show*

ELEANOR WAS AN ACTRESS who for years had sought for an
unknown something that she was never able to define. In
fact, so intense did this longing become at one time that
she consulted her physician. The intensity of her hunger
had caused an empty feeling within that she actually
thought was physical and could be cured by an operation.

The doctor informed Eleanor that he was not able to operate on spiritual problems.

The cause of her deep-seated hunger went back to early childhood. Before she was two years old, her parents had been divorced, and shortly afterward her mother disappeared. Her whereabouts has never been known. Eleanor was left to the care of a grandmother who desired for her a career on the stage. By the time Eleanor was only four she and her grandmother had moved to California and were working hard to break into the movies. Dancing lessons were the order of the day.

Because she was exceptionally beautiful, it was not long before Eleanor had the coveted contract. Her early success distorted her sense of values completely, and she never was a good student in school. She said, "I lived in a world of fantasy. I could see no purpose in study, for I was already earning big money for a girl. But grandmother couldn't be satisfied. She arranged for music lessons, and I found myself studying harp and voice.

"By the time I was twenty-three," she went on, "I had a musical contract in New York. Grandmother kept telling me how much I owed her for my success. I came to resent her terribly and we fought often. I was also concerned about all the girls getting married, and it seemed to me to be the thing to do. A very fine guy proposed marriage, but when we were finally married, I was unable to express love or give myself completely. I was fearful of being hurt, so I rejected his love. My thinking was all mixed up. We had a lovely daughter, and because I couldn't love my husband as I felt I should, I urged divorce so that my daugh-

ter could have a better home with my husband. That
seemed to be the answer. I wanted to be a good wife and
mother but I simply wasn't able emotionally.

"All of this was more than I could bear. Having separated from my husband and twelve-year-old daughter, and
then constantly quarreling with grandmother, I began to
drink. I cannot describe the horrible loneliness I experienced. Yes, I did have a contract, but that solved no
emotional problem. I would begin the contract with terrible fears over what would happen when it was over. My
feelings were that there was nobody who could help me.
You see I didn't at that time know Jesus. More than once
I seriously considered suicide. But I was even afraid to die.
Though I had thought of myself as a Christian when a
young girl, it had been years since I had been in a church.
I was without any knowledge of the Bible. I didn't know
that it had any message for a person like myself.

"It was when I was so disturbed and filled with all kinds
of fear that I received a call from a young man asking me
to visit the Billy Graham Crusade. He sent me reserved
seat tickets, and that made me want to go. I had no idea
what to expect. There had been much talk about Billy
Graham among show people, and they all were puzzled
over the crowds. With all of our know-how we had never
been able to equal anything like that. I was very curious
as I went to observe and listen.

"That night Billy preached on the loneliness of sin. I
knew I was lonely, desperately lonely and afraid. I was
not conscious of any spiritual struggle, but felt all over
again an agonizing loneliness. As he was preaching, I

seemed more lonely than I had ever been. I was alone in a crowd of twenty thousand.

"I had heard some of my colleagues tell about the invitation and I had even read in the paper about people going forward, but I never knew until that night what it all meant. I thought it was some strange religious form peculiar to Billy. Billy said, 'Come now, you may never have another chance.' I grabbed my seat and hung on. It was a physical thing with me. I'll never forget it, because it was so unlike me to get involved in anything like that. Besides, I still didn't understand what going down to the front would do for me. Right while I was most certain that I would not yield, I suddenly got up and started. I felt as though the chair had been wired. Suddenly I became like putty. I forgot my pride and stopped resisting. I ran as if I were afraid I wouldn't make it.

"That night, the first time I had ever heard the Gospel, I was born a new person in Christ. Once I got down in the counseling room, I had very little emotion. It was over by then. From the Bible, one of the wonderful counselors, a young girl, showed me the way to Christ. I went that way. I not only found Christ, but I finally found myself. The terrible loneliness was gone and it has never returned. I am not afraid any more. I am really the most carefree person in the world."

Eleanor went home that night a new person. She didn't think that others would notice it. The following day when she went to the restaurant where she usually ate her dinner, the waiter came to take her order. This time she ordered no drinks. The bartender looked over at her in amazement. He turned to the manager, a kindly Jewish man, and said, "It won't last." The owner came to the table where she was sitting and said, "Thank God. I pitied you when you came in here to drink alone. I am so glad something has happened to you." Something had happened to her, and she gladly told the owner of the restaurant of her new way. Thoughtfully he listened, and wondered at the transformation that had taken place since she had been there just two days before in the throes of alcohol. God had wrought the miracle of regeneration. She was a new creation. Old things had passed away, and behold all had become new.

A half year has already passed, and Eleanor is happy in her decision. She has come to know the privilege of walking with God. There is much that is still new, as there is for all who make their decisions for Christ. But life has begun, and it is true that "He which hath begun a good work in you will perform it until the day of Jesus."

Ardith and Dan were two of the innumerable couples living in an attractive apartment along famous Riverside Drive, overlooking the Henry Hudson Parkway and the Hudson River. Unknown to many who sat with them one evening at the Billy Graham Crusade in Madison Square Garden, they were both well known in the world of entertainment. She was an all-time popular singer in one of New York's fashionable night clubs, and he would be recognized to watchers of one of the outstanding TV comedy programs.

It would be difficult to convey to another the joy that was so evident in both of their lives as they told another story of the mysterious ways of God in influencing those who are to inherit salvation. Now that they had come to experience the cleansed conscience so well known to believers in Christ, they recalled one event after another in the past that had finally brought them both to the cross of Christ where they were led to lay down a burden of sin. The prophet Isaiah had spoken of the great king Cyrus, ". . . I girded thee, though thou has not known me" (Isaiah 45:5). It is the experience of many others who have recognized the gracious guidance of God during the years when no thought was given to His ways.

While Ardith was preparing a delicious dinner, Dan began to tell the story of his experiences in the past. He had been born in the West, and had all the physical appearance of a man's man. Standing six feet four inches, and weighing nearly 250 pounds, he made his five-foot wife look exceptionally small. There was a congenial wholesomeness about his manner that was winning and pleasant. Although for twenty-seven years he had lived without hope and without God, he did not bear the marks of sin as so many do. He was one of those clean-cut men one likes to meet. In fact, he was one of those whom many would not consider a candidate for salvation, for he had lived an exemplary life.

Dan could not remember any religious influence at home. Though his parents were fine people, they had never had a sense of spiritual values to pass on to their children. Having great ambition and more than his share

of physical prowess, Dan had fixed his mind on a career
of heavyweight boxing. As soon as school days were over,
he left his home in Nebraska to seek fame and fortune in
the prize ring. When he arrived in California, he first went
to observe some of the top fighters at work. He looked
them over carefully, and realized that to get to the top he
would have to knock out the best of them. This realization
caused him to renounce such a career before it had ever
begun.

Then came a good chance to travel to New York. Dan
had always longed to see the Big City with its excitement
and "bright lights." With a friend he traveled across the
continent and finally arrived in one of the world's most
exciting cities. He had quite forgotten his urge to enter
the boxing ring. Now the most exciting career seemed to
be in quite a different direction. He was still a very young
man, better than average in appearance, and definitely an
eligible bachelor. As he stood looking over Rockefeller
Plaza, as most tourists do when they come to New York,
a beautiful and aggressive young lady came by and engaged him in conversation. She seemed to be just one part
of the unfolding of an exciting drama. She influenced him
to remain in New York when he had actually planned to
return to his home in the western plains. She also directed
him to the stage and the entertainment world. Although
she soon dropped out of his life, she had entered it at a
strategic moment.

Once he had made his way into the entertainment
world, Dan went from one show to another with outstanding success. After playing a few small parts, he joined

a stock company, traveling across the Southland. It was the drama of Daniel Boone, acted out on the very trail over which the famous pioneer had traveled more than a century before. Dan's part in this show was the frontier preacher, whose only book was the Bible and whose message was a message of hell-fire and brimstone for the wicked and heaven for the redeemed.

In Asheville, North Carolina, Dan met another young woman who was to have a part in his story. She gave him a Bible. It was the first one he had owned, and he planned to use it in acting his part as the backwoods preacher. He then told of its effect on his thoughts.

"I used to sit backstage and read the Bible. I thought it was the part of a good actor to identify himself with the role he was playing. I had never had formal training in drama, but I had always liked to act. I knew that a good actor must actually 'become' the character he is playing. I was trying to be a true backwoods preacher.

"A strange thing was happening to me. The more I read the Bible, the more it impressed me. Moreover, the writer of the play script had evidently done considerable research on the sermons of backwoods preachers. I found myself calling on the rugged pioneers to repent and believe the Bible. I warned them to flee from the wrath to come. I wouldn't admit it to a single person, but my part really scared me. Many times I wondered if all this might be true. What I had to learn from the script was also in the Bible. I never really got away from that experience. My part in the Daniel Boone play had made a lasting impression on my life.

"Back again in New York after that show had completed its run, I went from one show to another. Every once in a while I was cast in a religious part.

"Show people are a gregarious lot and when we get together we naturally talk shop. At one of these get-togethers I was introduced to the girl who was to become my wife. I liked everything about her and didn't waste any time making the first date with her. She seemed different from so many show people I had met. I found out that she was a singer at a night club. She seemed to be much too refined and cultured for that kind of singing.

"Before long we were married. We had so many things in common and had such a lot of things to enjoy together it seemed just right for us to get married. She was even religious, like I was. We went to church once in a while, but never did identify ourselves with any particular one. The way it was, we just went when we happened to wake up early enough on Sunday morning, and when it didn't interfere with any plans we might have."

All the time Dan was telling this story, Ardith was bringing the food to the table. This was their one night of the week to be home together, and she showed her real love for homemaking. Every trip between the kitchen and living room was punctuated with her comments on the great spiritual discovery they had made. Suddenly life had taken on new meaning for both of them. Even their relationship as husband and wife had undergone a change. They now were experiencing the presence of the risen Lord in the commonplace affairs of life.

Ardith looked with true affection at Dan when she interrupted his story to tell how she first met him. She knew that she felt toward him as she had never felt toward any young man before. She said, "He looked at me in a way no other man had looked at me. He was so clean and wholesome. It was not a look of passion but more of admiration. It was such a relief to talk to someone who wasn't a wolf. Well, from that meeting on, we just got together every chance we had, and it wasn't long before we were married. We were happy all of the time with each other, but we never knew how much more there was to life.

"You see," Ardith continued, "we were both striving to get to the top in our careers. Even before I met Dan, I had studied voice with some of the leading teachers in New York. When I had finally satisfied my teacher, the plans were made for my debut at Carnegie Hall. I was looking forward to this night.

"In one way, at least, I wasn't much different from any other student. I was perpetually broke. To pay for my lessons and other expenses was more than I could manage. I had just six weeks to go before my concert. Right then I was offered a chance to go on the road with a vaudeville troupe. It offered good pay, and my mother encouraged me to go. It was an exciting six weeks and I got the money I needed so badly. The trouble was, I had damaged my voice and my voice teacher cancelled my concert. It was a long time before I was able to sing again, and when my voice finally came back, I had lost my only chance to enter the career of an opera singer.

Just when success was in front of me, I made a wrong decision. At least it seemed wrong then. Now I know that all such decisions I can leave with the Lord and trust His guidance. I didn't know Him then and assumed all the responsibility myself. That is why I am singing in a night club and not in opera today."

Most of the people of the entertainment world are on the alert for anything as unusual as a show that will fill Madison Square Garden. They are even more interested in any person who can command such an audience night after night. Dan and Ardith wanted to attend the service at the Garden at least once. On their first free night they made their first visit and became two more of the thousands who returned night after night.

Dan's interest in religion dated back to the days when he had played the part of the backwoods preacher, but his chief motive in visiting the Garden was to observe a man who could sway multitudes. He did not realize that he was to hear more than just a man speaking; he was to hear an ambassador of Jesus Christ. He would listen to the Word of God with ears he had not used before, with the ears of his soul.

Ardith too was to hear a message that would change the entire direction of her life. She had been career-conscious all of her life. This experience, she thought, was going to add something to her ability as a career person. They sat together intending to enjoy a demonstration that at least was something different. Then a strange thing happened. However, it was not strange to those who knew the power of God and to those who had watched the moving of the Holy Spirit during those memorable nights at the Garden.

"But when Billy began to preach," Dan explained, "we were both suddenly aware of the fact that something was happening to us that we couldn't explain. I was reminded of my role as the preacher, but of course Billy was different. The Bible he used was the same, and some of the verses were the same. I felt a power working in my soul that I couldn't resist. I looked at my wife, and I knew she also was feeling the effects of the Word as Billy preached. It was an experience we couldn't describe.

"I had always taken great pride in my morality and ethical way of life. Both Ardith and I felt quite secure in our love for each other. But Billy was making us both feel and know that in reality we were far away from God. It was a feeling of something missing in our lives. It's really wonderful that He spoke to us both. Since then we have heard of so many couples who had the experience of one or the other coming to Christ, but with us it was a joint decision. I don't know why the Lord should have been so good to us."

Those who make their decision in the Billy Graham Crusades are usually affected in a similar manner. As they listen to the preaching of the Word, they find that before long they have quite forgotten the speaker. As the Holy Spirit directs the living Word to their hearts, they become conscious of His presence and power in a way they cannot describe. Before their coming to Christ this couple had experienced a oneness in their marriage that few persons enjoy, but the fulness of that relationship

cannot be discovered until another Person is brought into
it. That is what Dan and Ardith found the night they
sat and listened.

As he continued talking about that wonderful night and
all it had come to mean to them both, Dan recalled that,
"As Billy continued his sermon and neared the time for
the invitation, I was almost afraid to look at Ardith.
Somehow I knew that I must make my decision that
night. I was afraid that I would have to do it alone. We
hadn't talked much about religion, and so I didn't know
for sure what Ardith was thinking."

Ardith had been thinking back over her own life and
its disappointments. She had grown up in the home of an
alcoholic father. As a girl she had never had the feeling of
security a child needs. Only when she and Dan were
married did she feel that someone cared for and wanted
her. Now she thought as she listened, "If I make my decision for Christ, and Dan doesn't, what will it do to the
wonderful life we have had together as husband and
wife?"

The invitation time finally came, and as always, Billy
called for men and women everywhere in that great building to come forward. Everyone sensed the mysterious
power of the Spirit of God, and in a special way Dan and
Ardith felt His presence. Then without more than a
moment of hesitation, they left their seats.

Together they walked to the front of Madison Square
Garden to receive Christ as their Saviour and Lord. There
was a new joy in their lives that night. Some who do not
know the ways of the Lord would have said it couldn't

last. Others would have said that they were just fleeing from reality. But they knew that God had done something miraculous in their souls, and that they could never be the same. A change had taken place that the natural man cannot comprehend.

Many who read the story of Dan and Ardith will soon wonder how far-reaching that change was in their lives. As the leisurely dinner progressed, and we all were enjoying the wonderful food she had prepared, Ardith began to tell what deep feelings she had. "As I review my own life, I can see how God was allowing things to happen to me to prepare me for this hour. Our home problem when I was a little girl . . . my vocal training and career . . . meeting Dan. This all has been part of it. I have been singing at this night club for a while now. The owner has been wonderful to me, and I cannot complain about the work, but I feel that this voice is the one talent God has given me to give back to Him. I can choose the songs I sing every night. Often I sing by request. But I feel that I want more than anything else to sing for the Lord. What do you think I should do about this?"

Then Dan began to ask questions about his own career. "How do you know when the Lord calls you into the ministry? Is there any way that He speaks so that you don't make mistakes? I enjoy my acting, and all the shows I do are clean and wholesome. But it seems that God must have something more important for me to do than to entertain." These were the problems that were discussed that evening. The problems are important, but it is also important to see what a complete revolution has taken place in the

lives of Dan and Ardith, a revolution that cannot be explained by those who speak of conversion as nothing more
than an emotional spasm. Only a work of God could have
changed their desires and rendered such changes perma-
nent. The very essence of the conversion experience is the
shift from a devotion to one's self to a devotion to God.
When once the appetite for worldly acclaim is lost, a deep
desire for complete devotion to God is experienced.

Such complete devotion is frequently exemplified in the
lives of those who find the way. Mary was one of those
who by her very nature would be devoted to someone or
to some cause. For that reason, the formality of the religion of her parents failed to satisfy her deeper longings.
She sometimes went with them to Mass, but felt that such
formality lacked relevance and reality. Her parents, who
were not too firmly attached to their own church, did not
object when she chose to attend another one. Her church
provided her with little knowledge of the Bible.

Mary was an aesthetic individual, appreciating all that
is beautiful and artistic. On one occasion she saw a Russian ballet. This artistic demonstration appealed to her
sensitive spirit. There was an appeal in such artistry, and
this was associated in her thinking with communism. After
a futile attempt to reconcile the existence of God with
communistic philosophy, she turned to communism as a
serious study. One of her close girl friends was a communist student, and thus she was drawn into the movement.

Mary's girl friend was her ideal. She was aesthetic and

intelligent. But she had not found the answer to the many problems of life. On one occasion her friend had attempted suicide. This unsuccessful attempt caused Mary to think more seriously than ever about the problems of life. Some time later this friend died, leaving an empty void in Mary's life.

This experience was followed by an experiment in love. Mary met a man considerably older than herself. She was nineteen at the time, and he had already been married for some time. There was a glamour about being invited out by a mature man. She was flattered by his attention. Knowing that he was married gave her a guilty feeling, but she was so enamoured of him that she could not break off with him.

Mary had chosen the stage as her career. At the time the Billy Graham Crusade began, she was in the London University theater school as a student. She related, "Many of the students there were talking about this American evangelist. We decided to attend some of the meetings to observe this unusual speaker. All the time I studied the communistic philosophy, I knew there was something better. I did not expect to hear it from an American evangelist. I was in pursuit of the truth wherever I might find it. I had always hoped for an answer.

"This message I heard from Billy that night was just the one for me. His text, I recall, was from Isaiah 1:18: 'Come now, and let us reason together, saith the Lord. . . .' This made an immediate impression upon me. I had never heard the text before, and God's call to come and reason appealed to me. Billy was authoritative and earnest.

Even the communists I had heard lacked the conviction and commitment I saw in him.

"I remember that on the day before we went to hear him, I had found a clipping describing his London meetings when he had been there the first time. I haven't the slightest idea how I ever got it, but it heightened my interest in him. I believe that even this little incident had some bearing upon the decision I was to make that very night. Then to see his earnestness that night made me feel as if I were not myself.

"While Billy was giving the invitation, I waited. I really didn't intend to do anything about Christ that night. I pondered the cost of discipleship as I had once done before when I was a student of communism. I felt numb. I kept asking myself how I could live this life. Its demands were for total commitment. At the same time I was sincerely repentant for wrongs I had done. I had always thought of myself as being good, and by worldly standards I had been, but that night I received a new conception of sin. It was sin of such magnitude that it called for the death of Christ to atone for it. All of this I could not resist, and finally, when the invitation was nearly over, I went to make known my desire to know Christ as my own personal Saviour and Lord.

"A very nice girl counseled me, but I was not impressed with her. I had loved clothes and beautiful things. She was extremely plain, and I wondered if I would come to that. Somehow I forgot her plainness in a few seconds, for she was very devoted to Christ and knew her Bible well. But I had read and studied too many other world views to consider her answers as final that night. But somehow, as she showed me the Word of God and prayed for me, the change came and I was born anew. Everything was different. For me, it was the end of a long search. I felt that at last I had found what I had been seeking for so long.

"Things began to happen in rapid succession. Back at the theater school there was a great deal of talk about Billy Graham. Some of the other students had been changed as I had. This distressed our leaders greatly. Within a matter of a few weeks, it was evident that everything was to be different. Even my love affair was to be broken by this decision. My friend was not in agreement with me when I told him what had happened to me. As we parted I felt like a ship setting sail, with him left standing on the shore.

"At school those of us who were converted discussed whether we should continue in the theater. Some converts we knew had acted suddenly and had not completed their schooling. I decided to finish my formal training for the theater. In fact, I was not opposed to the theater at once. But at the very time I was about to begin my career, I felt the Lord definitely leading me into special Christian service. I'm so grateful today for the direction I received at that time."

Since that night, Mary's life has been one filled with drama and thrills, but it has all been in the glorious leading of God. Nearly three years of industrial evangelism, and now service with the Navigators, a Christian soulwinning movement, have claimed her time and energy. Mary has been used in directing many to the knowledge of

Christ. She has come to be well known to members of the team as a winner of souls and an able teacher of the Bible. Her service in directing Bible study groups has effectively conserved the fruits of evangelism on both sides of the Atlantic. She represents the commitment to Christ that is called for in the words of the Saviour who said, "If any man will come after me, let him take up his cross and follow me."

Actors and actresses are suddenly confronted with problems that are foreign to most people who make their decisions for Christ. In accepting a new way of life, they are often confronted with the problem of their careers. Each individual must make his own private decision in the matter. These people of glamour and lights are often looked upon with suspicion by those who know little or nothing about such problems. One Christian leader expressed wonder when he heard of the conversion of a London actress during the Billy Graham London Crusade. But today that beautiful and talented girl is walking in fellowship with Christ. Her story may well tell the future of many actresses who came forward at the New York Crusade.

Joan was once called "The prettiest girl in England." She has lost none of that beauty. The change that took place and has continued since the great London Crusade has enhanced that natural beauty by giving to it a spiritual quality, " . . . that which is not corruptible, even the ornament of a meek and quiet spirit, which is in the sight of

God of great price." Physical charm is known to disappear with age, but the loveliness of spirit which is renewed daily through the Word of God and prayer is a beauty that every woman can have, and Joan has this beauty.

The seed of the Word of God was sown in her heart as a very young girl. Because of her mother's death when Joan was only four years of age, she was sent to a private school to study. School days were over when she was sixteen, and then came business training and finally a position as a secretary. This position brought her in contact with the theater business. Because of her unusual beauty she was soon playing minor parts, even though she had no formal training in the art of acting.

From the beginning she was aware of the conflict in certain theatrical productions and the religious life. But by a process of rationalizing, she was able to convince herself that God would understand. As she grew more and more popular and was in greater demand, she was drawn away from the church and its religious influences.

She said, "I was afraid of people and would not mention Christ or religion. I knew I should not forsake the church entirely. Often I intended going to church, but unless everything worked out conveniently, I just didn't make it. Along with growing popularity and success was a growing sense of spiritual need. I was becoming miserable with it all.

"I made my big picture, and was presented to the royal family who came to see the picture. This was indeed a great honor to me, as it would be to anyone in my pro-

fession. I was also doing more and more television work.
If worldly success could make a person happy, I should
have been happy, but I was becoming desperate in my
search for an inward composure and peace.

"During the war I met many soldiers, and in company
with them I began to drink considerably. I could feel myself slipping into a very low kind of life, yet I didn't have
the strength to do a single thing about it. I felt I was
being pushed around without the ability to resist.

"I believe that my early religious training took me
through all this horrible experience. When Billy Graham
came to London to conduct the Crusade, I had just come
through two serious nervous breakdowns. Now I think I
can explain them, but at that time I couldn't control my
emotions at all. Then I had been passing through months
of misery. One day a friend asked me to join her in going
to Harringay to hear Billy Graham. At first I resented an
American coming to preach to us, but my curiosity got
the better of me. I felt an irresistible urge to go that I
have not been able to explain until recently. Now I know
that a dear saint of God in far-off Australia had been praying for me over a year without my knowledge. The ways
of God are quite beyond us, aren't they?

"That night at Harringay I listened to the testimony of
Dale Evans and listened to Billy Graham. All through the
service I thought of my career. I was afraid. For a long
time I had been running from problems, and now again
I felt like running away from them. I had always been
torn between pleasing God and pleasing men, and I always
reasoned that God would understand because I did cer-

tain things to get on in the world. Now I was face to face with God.

"As Billy preached, he told so clearly and forthrightly how Christ had gone to the cross for my sin. I had always thought of Him dying for the world's sin, but not for mine personally. Now I heard that He died for me. Before this night I had been on the verge of suicide, but as I listened I somehow knew that Christ was the answer to my problem. I could no longer compromise, but I must give my life completely to Him.

"I am grateful to God that I had to get up out of my seat and walk down that long aisle, for until then I had always been ashamed of letting people know anything about my religious belief. I have known Christ for more than three years now, and I can honestly say that they have been the richest and most joyful years of my life. I used to get distressed when, after my conversion, self would rise up and I would fail. Realization that the Christian life is a gradual growth has helped me so much.

"I shall never forget the one show I did after I had found the Saviour. I was desperately in need of money at the time, and a contract was offered that was very attractive. I foolishly signed it without so much as reading the script. Afterwards I read it and was shocked to find that it was actually the worst picture of my career. I wondered how I could get out of it, for it was not becoming to a Christian. I begged to be released but they would not release me. I had to go on with the picture.

"One day some of the press men came to get a story about it. They wanted to write up a story on what happens

to the converts of the Billy Graham meetings. I explained
what a foolish thing I had done, and begged them not to
write the story. I would surely have given the world the
wrong idea. I was ashamed of my part in a show that was
substandard. But I was thankful for one thing. It convinced me that I would have no future in the movies. As a
Christian I felt I could not continue. That was my last
picture, and I'm sure the Lord has forgiven the silly decision of one who was so recently converted. It was definitely the mistake of one who had not yet come to know
the Lord in His fulness nor to know well His Word.

"I am happily married to a wonderful Christian now,
and since the birth of our son, I have learned many lessons
in growth that can be applied to the Christian life. I did
not formerly understand what Jesus meant when He said,
'Except ye be converted; and become as little children
. . . .' I am beginning to understand this as I watch my
son and see his unquestioning faith in and love for my
husband and me. I saw him fall often while learning to
walk, just as I fell in the early days of my spiritual walk
with the Lord.

"Jesus Christ has filled my life completely with His
love and grace, and has given me a husband with whom I
am an heir of the grace of life to come. No matter what
may happen as far as the world is concerned, we have the
assurance that one day we shall see His face and be with
Him forever—what peace of mind we can have in these
troubled days. It is a peace that for so long I sought and
finally found in the Billy Graham Crusade at Harringay
Arena in London in 1954. When Billy Graham introduced

me to Jesus Christ, instead of taking my own life, I gave it to Him."

During the sixteen weeks of the New York Crusade some four hundred people in this fabulous world of bright lights made their decisions for Jesus Christ.

5. Religion that Failed

MILDRED WAS ONE of thousands who told of her attendance at church when in her younger years. In America there are only a few who have had no church affiliations. Almost ninety per cent of our people attended some church at some time and more than sixty per cent claim to hold membership in some denominations. Pastors know how little this means to the Christian life of many, but when the story of conversion is told, there is usually some reference to the church that was visited upon occasions in the past.

In Mildred's case she attended church with her family. In fact she was forced to go with her mother and stepfather. They were active in the work of the church, but Mildred somehow "never took to it," as she expressed it. The one activity she remembered was Sunday school.

"I had a very nice Sunday school teacher. She used to thrill us with her vivid telling of Bible stories. She could make the characters of the Old Testament live before us. As I recall it, she never did do more than familiarize us with these characters, and no special lesson was drawn from the account. I definitely remember one great disappointment I had in her class. I think it was the turning point for me because after that time I somehow lost interest in religion.

"It happened on one of those Sunday mornings when we were listening to her tell a Bible story. The week before I had done something I knew was wrong, and my conscience was bothering me. So I asked her about wrong and about sin. She gave me no answer at all but ignored me. She seemed very annoyed with my question. I didn't ask again because I knew I must have done something that annoyed her.

"When I didn't get an answer to that question I began to justify my actions by comparing myself with the other girls I knew in the church. We talked about different things as young girls do, and after a while I became convinced that to be as good as the others was the most anyone could expect."

All of this happened during the years that Mildred was growing up to young womanhood. There in a small Indiana town, where life was free and wholesome, she had developed a wrong system of ethics that was to show up when she was thrown into the maelstrom of temptation in the big city. As she matured, she became the neat, efficient professional girl, so typical of the busy offices in lower Manhattan. After ten years of New York life, she bore little resemblance to the girl who had left Indiana. She was sophisticated and worldly wise, possessed a tremendous vitality that made her a fascinating person.

"When I first came to New York," she said, "I had a lovely roommate. As long as we lived together, I enjoyed the city. We had many things in common, and until she married, everything went along quite well. Five years ago she met and married a fine young man. Since then I have been living alone in the same small apartment. You have no idea how lonely you get in this big city when you are living alone. In the midst of millions of people, you are still alone. After just so much of that awful loneliness you begin to think and do strange things. Day after day in the office I would meet nice people and work with them. But when I stepped off the elevator on the ground floor and passed through that revolving door into the street, they disappeared in the crowd and I was alone again. It's a terrible kind of loneliness.

"That sort of thing gets you after a while. There was a very influential man who came to my desk almost every day on business. He was fine looking and very friendly. One day he asked me to have dinner with him. I was glad for the invitation because it was a change from the old routine. Until we had that first dinner together, I had been planning to go back to Indiana. I had written my family that I was coming. But there was an attraction about this man that made me stay. I couldn't resist him. We began going out regularly, and I forgot my plans to go home.

"After a few dates he told me about himself, and to my

surprise I learned that he was married. I should have guessed that, but I suppose one has a way of refusing to think about certain things. At least I did. What puzzles me now is that for some reason, our relationship didn't seem wrong. I liked it so much, and he was kind to me. I just rationalized about the thing and made it all seem right.

"While going with him, I began drinking. First it was just the usual cocktail before dinner. It's quite the thing to do, you know. After a hectic day in an office, the tension builds you up, and by night you're ready to fly. Then you take a drink to settle your nerves and forget your problems. We did that regularly. I was really proud of the fact that I could take it or leave it. After a while I just accepted the fact that I needed that drink at the end of the day. I didn't want to admit it, but before long I couldn't do without it. I didn't want to believe I was near alcoholism, but I was. I guess when the time comes when you can't leave it alone, you must be alcoholic.

"Along with drinking went all the other intimacies that couples frequently experience. I enjoyed his company so much; the fact that he didn't mention his family helped me to forget that part of it. What bothered me most was that I always had to wait for him to call me. I could never call him lest his wife know he was being unfaithful. When he didn't call me, and especially on weekends, I would drop into a certain bar on the way home, and drink. I couldn't seem to think of anything else to do when he wasn't with me.

"During all this time I still would go to church. I knew

that I was not doing right, but then I would begin to compare my life with the others in the church. I would always say to myself, 'I'm not the best, but neither am I the worst one,' and that thought would give me some comfort. This certainly was a mixed-up life, but I knew others who were mixed up. I had come to think that this was the way life was. I just didn't have anything to take hold of. This was my life at the time Billy Graham began the great crusade."

Mildred then related how she had read about Billy Graham when he was preaching in London in 1953. She thought it unusual that a preacher should be given such recognition in the press and on the radio. But like many who read of that working of the Holy Spirit in Harringay, when there was no more news she temporarily forgot about it all. Only occasionally did she have a brief moment of religious concern which she would soon drown with liquor. She also told how circumstances had kept her in New York during these years, though she had often planned to return to her home.

In the course of her story Mildred said, "I believe I was kept here in New York to make the decision. Life has a plan, and I was meant to stay here. Billy often told us that no one was here by accident. We were all here by divine appointment. At first I thought it was a strange thing to say, but when I began to put together the broken pieces of my life, it all made sense. God had planned it that way.

"When I began to hear about Billy Graham coming to New York, my interest was renewed. I first went to the

great Forest Hills meeting. There I was actually frightened. So many things were passing through my mind, and
the more he spoke the more I knew I'd have to go forward.
When he gave the invitation, I resisted. I just wasn't going
to follow a crowd. I was afraid of getting drawn into a
mass movement, so I went home after the meeting without any decision being made.

"I arrived home with the memory of that meeting still
fresh in my mind. I forgot all about the usual stop in the
bar for a drink. My mind was going in circles. I went to
bed still thinking of the message and of my own resistance
to it. I even wondered why I was inclined to respond at
all, and then I would wonder why I hadn't answered the
call. I was never more restless or troubled in my life. As
I rolled and tossed on my bed, something kept saying to
me, 'You were very foolish tonight.' I just couldn't get
that out of my mind. Here was the offer of inward peace
for which I had sought. Here was the answer to my girlish
question that a Sunday school teacher had not answered.
I reviewed my whole life and saw all that was wrong with
it. The more I thought about it, the more restless I
became.

"Finally at four o'clock in the morning I said, 'It's now
or never.' The burden of my past life had finally become
too great, and my problems were too complex for me to
solve by myself. Right then I got out of bed and got on
my knees before God. I knew what I must do, because
Billy had made that point clear. He had been throwing
Scripture at me through the whole message.

"I didn't know if the same thing would happen to me

in the loneliness of my room that happened to the people who decided at a meeting. At first I was afraid to ask God to save me. I guess I thought that it had to happen at the time the invitation was given. But I soon found out. I confessed every sin I could think of and most of all the sin of refusing to recognize Christ as the only Saviour from sin and self.

"Billy had been telling about being born again. One thing I was sure of was that I had never had anything like that take place. I was the same sinful Mildred I had always been. Then it happened. I don't know how to explain to you what took place, but right while I was confessing my terrible need, and asking God for help, I was mysteriously led to put my whole trust in Christ. I was helped to rely on what He had done for sinners. When I did that, a wonderful peace that I had never known came over me, and it hasn't left me from that early morning hour on June 11th until right now. God has wonderfully transformed my whole life.

"The following night I was ready to go to the Garden; I didn't even care whether my boy friend called or not. I went to the meeting and when the invitation came, I went forward. I knew what I was doing—I was making a public stand for the Saviour who had already done so much for me. Billy preached that night on the necessity of acknowledging Christ openly. One of the verses Billy pressed home so often says, 'If thou shalt confess with thy mouth the Lord Jesus, and shalt believe in thine heart that God hath raised him from the dead, thou shalt be saved.' That night was really a dedication of myself to

Christ to witness for Him, and I have done so ever since.

"The first experience I had with witnessing was about two days after my decision. My boy friend called me and asked me to have lunch with him. I was very nervous about it. I didn't know how it would work out. Billy had mentioned once that you don't need to worry about your friends because the Lord would take care of that. Well, He certainly did. I met him at lunch time, and we began to talk. On the phone he said he had something to tell me, and I answered that I had something to tell him too. This was my chance. He said to me, 'What was it you wanted to tell me?' I began to tell the story of my acceptance of Christ and the change in my life. As I spoke to him, he began to weep. He said he was very happy for me, and that I had done a wonderful thing. I told him that it would make a difference in our relationship.

"As we were talking and eating together, he offered me a cigarette, but I refused. I don't even know why because I don't remember ever having thought about it. I didn't even take a drink. In fact, I had prayed about my appetite for liquor because I knew that was something I couldn't handle. Now I didn't even want it. I know that he must have realized that a complete change had taken place, because he has never called me since. He comes by the office on business now and then, but acts as if he had scarcely known me. I hope he realizes that he needs the Lord just as much as I do."

The young Christian experiences a kind of temptation that is typical of all who are so recently brought into the fellowship of believers. The temptation is to return to the old life from which they have so recently been redeemed.

Mildred had also experienced this temptation. She recalled that it came to her with unusual force the day of the great meeting at Yankee Stadium. She was among the thousands who sat there in the heat of a July sun from early afternoon until evening. There were no refreshments available, and to leave a seat meant never to get it again.

After sitting there during the hours that the great stadium was being filled, and then through the thrilling meeting when more than five thousand persons made their stand for Christ, she was extremely thirsty. She went home as usual on the subway. At the end of the subway line was the tavern where she had stopped so many times. There was the old crowd and for a moment an overwhelming desire for a cold glass of beer was more than she could resist in her own strength. But suddenly, she recalled, "A power greater than myself enabled me to go past the door and on to my apartment. I have never had that particular temptation since. I walk by the place every night and don't even notice it any more. Isn't it wonderful what God will do for us when we really want Him to?"

Some find it necessary to leave their former occupations when they turn to Christ. A middle-aged woman who had worked for the "bookies" couldn't go back to work the next day. Mildred's work was legitimate and did not call for a change. In fact it provided the very best place for her to be a living example of what Christ does in the lives of those who are influenced by Him. She admitted that she had formerly been very irritable and easily ruffled. She had been indifferent to her work.

She said, "The change in my disposition is confusing all

the men in the office. They notice that I just don't get
ruffled any more. They stop and ask what has happened,
and that gives me the perfect opportunity to tell what
Christ can do for you. I always had it in my mind that
God would forgive you if you asked, but I had never heard
about the changed life. I don't think they have ever heard
of it either, because they are completely baffled when I
turn down a drink or refuse a date with one of them. One
of the men in the office, a Roman Catholic, stopped one
day and quietly expressed his admiration. He said that he
would have to admit that Graham must have something.
Of course I quickly told him that it was the Lord who had
done so much for me.

"And it's sort of funny. I have a new ambition I never
had before. I take real pride in my work. The boss stopped
by the other day and told me that for some time he had
noticed that I was slipping. He was greatly concerned and
even had considered replacing me. He told me that although he didn't understand this matter of conversion, he
said I had overnight become the best secretary he had
ever had."

Mildred was doing what the believer is admonished in
the Word of God, "Servants, be obedient to them that are
your masters according to the flesh, with fear and trem-
bling, in singleness of your heart, as unto Christ; Not with
eyeservice, as menpleasers; but as the servants of Christ,
doing the will of God from the heart" (Ephesians 6:5,6).

The new-found relationship to Christ has had its effect
on other aspects of living for Mildred too. Before she had
felt this awful loneliness, of which many other girls com-

plained, but now she says, "I'm not lonely any more. I have a constant companion in Christ. Besides, I have found wonderful Christian friends I never knew anything about before. My conversion has even had some effect on the church. I went to the pastor and asked if we might have a prayer meeting. He was a very discouraged man before. He said he would be more than glad to do so. He never thought the people wanted to pray. The next Sunday he announced a prayer meeting, and a large number came. We now have regular prayer meetings. The pastor has a new enthusiasm I never believed he would have. There is real power in the meeting, and we are praying for many in the church who don't know Christ. The pastor is preaching very definitely that men must be born again. It's really a wonderful experience.

"Yes, and I'm having some wonderful experiences helping in High School work with Hi-B.A. That's an organization in the High Schools of the Eastern half of the United States. Brandt Reed is such an inspiration to work with, and kids are being converted regularly. It makes me feel as though I'm in the Lord's work. Brandt told me I'd have to memorize a lot of Scripture to keep up with teen-agers. I just didn't believe I could do it. I thought I was too old to begin to memorize. I'm forty-five, and I just couldn't imagine keeping up with those kids. But the Lord has helped me, and believe it or not, I'm memorizing Scripture and getting the greatest blessing of my life."

And so changes take place one after another. Each story presents its own thrill and challenge. Each person has his personal problem and each one knows the blessing of

God's presence in his life. This is a transformation that stops the mouth of the most severe critic. The new life in Christ Jesus is the answer to the doubts and uncertainty of our times.

An entire section of Madison Square Garden had been reserved for clergymen of various denominations. Night after night the section was filled with men who were religious leaders. Some were from non-liturgical churches and others represented highly liturgical forms of religion. There were Presbyterians seated with Pentecostalists; Baptists seated with Episcopalians; Methodists and Lutherans were there with Jews and Greek Orthodox. Priests and rabbis were there to observe a religious service different from any kind of gathering in the church's history.

Together these religious leaders heard the Gospel songs, and some joined in singing such favorites as "This Is My Story, This Is My Song," and "Amazing Grace, How Sweet the Sound." Many participated in the meeting while some had come merely to observe. Whatever it was that brought them all together, they all felt the power and persuasion of the message in song and sermon. More impressive than everything else to these clergymen and religious leaders was the response to the invitation. Some were able to explain every other part of the service, but the spontaneous response to the invitation defied explanation. Whatever they thought of Billy Graham and his methods, there were the results in decisions before their eyes night after night.

As they observed, some rejoiced to see what they had not had faith to believe could come to pass. Men of God recognized the power of the Holy Spirit and knew that a new birth was taking place in thousands of persons. A few were disturbed at such a mass movement and felt that it lacked something, although they could not define it. But most disturbing to some was the occasional clergyman who would leave his place and join the inquirers to declare his need of the Saviour. An Episcopalian rector, the wife of a Baptist evangelist, a Methodist minister, a Presbyterian theological student were typical of this group.

On a certain evening as the clergy sat in its section, one of the group started on his way to the front to declare his decision for Christ. Others of them had done the same, but this time it was one who had been skeptical and unbelieving. His clerical frock indicated a communion whose superiors had forbidden attendance, but there was an irresistible force compelling his attendance. He felt that he *must* go, though he was unable to tell why.

"What impressed me most," he said afterward, "was Billy's declaration that a man can be changed in a moment by trusting in the merits of Jesus Christ. He convinced me from the Bible that faith is essential, and that was a truth that had completely escaped me."

Joe Murphy had come to America from Ireland just a few years ago. His Irish brogue told who his ancestors were. "In Ireland," he said, "we were ignorant of the Bible and the truth I have learned this summer at the

Crusade. From the time I was an altar boy until I completed my preparation for the priesthood, I studied the Bible very little. Nor did I have any religious experience that caused me to enter the clergy. My parents, especially my mother, urged me to give my life for the church. It meant a certain status for them, and that is what many people seek in the church.

"During my days of training, my task was to learn the ritual and liturgy, but hardly any Bible study. When once I had been fully ordained I should have been satisfied, but there always seemed to be something lacking. Some things troubled me about my church, but I always knew that I shouldn't expect the visible church to have the perfection of the invisible one. That way I accounted for everything that I felt was not what it should be.

"I had been ministering in New York for some time when I learned of the coming of Billy Graham. I was already curious because I knew what a terrific impact he had made on all of Britain when he was in London just a couple of years ago. The people of my church were told not to attend. In fact, I too didn't think they should attend. I felt that I must go to the Garden to learn any secret Billy might have that he could command such an audience.

"The meeting had scarcely begun when I observed an enthusiasm that was something contagious. Then I wondered why my people had been forbidden to attend. There was nothing evil about it. All was done decently and in order. There was a dignity in spite of the fact that in this very building there had been rodeos, boxing matches, ice-skating exhibitions and circuses.

"When the preliminaries were over and Billy began to preach, I sensed a Presence I had not known before. Then the message itself impressed me deeply. He said that every man could have direct access to God through Jesus Christ. From the Scriptures he quoted the verse that says, 'For there is one God, and one mediator between God and men, the man Christ Jesus; Who gave himself a ransom for all. . . .' This I simply could not refute. This was the Gospel according to any translation or version of the Scriptures. It was this use of the Scriptures that was the deciding factor because I was put in the position of either accepting the authority of the Scriptures, or rejecting it. It was not a controversy with Billy Graham. By his use of the Scriptures, he removed himself from the center and put God and the Scriptures there instead.

"What I had always wanted, and what my church didn't afford, was personal assurance of salvation. My reason for answering the invitation was to secure that assurance and know that I was saved for eternity. When I got to the counseling room, I naturally didn't get much help. The questions I had to ask were quite beyond the counselor. He did impress me with some of the verses and his ability to find them—an ability which I did not yet have. Nor was that occasion filled with much emotion. The fact is, I now experience more emotion when I hear the Gospel and when I study the Scriptures than I did that night. It must have been the fear of what would happen that kept me from letting my emotions run that night. But I did receive the assurance of salvation, and for that I shall be eternally grateful to God for speaking through Billy Graham to me.

"I couldn't sleep that night. I had a problem that most converts do not have. I not only had a Saviour to receive but a religious order to do something about. But my decision had been made, by the grace of God, and He also gave me the courage to withdraw from the ministry. For the first time in my life I felt free—liberated. In fact, I can't get used to it after three months. The freedom to study and interpret the Scriptures is an experience that I had never known. Now, thank God, I can get my orders from the Saviour Himself through His blessed Word.

"Needless to say, I was defrocked. According to the church I was marked as a heretic. It is even more than being sent away from the church. It will mean alienation from my family. They were always so proud of me. Now they will be ashamed. So will all my relatives, many of them members of religious orders.

"I don't know what the Lord will have me do. I have a longing to preach His Word, but I still have many questions that must be answered. I have no doubt about my personal salvation, but I must become much more versed in the Scriptures before I can ever proclaim the message. It may be that the Lord will have me serve in some measure in helping others who were in the same darkness that I was. Next week I shall leave for England where I plan to work for a while with a minister. That will give me time and opportunity to reflect upon the total meaning of my decision. Of one thing I am sure, and that is that I am now a child of God and have no longer the fear of death in me."

Assurance of salvation is the desire of more than one

who is engaged in religious work, and the story of Joe Murphy is just one of many clergymen who joined laymen and sought forgiveness through the God-appointed means. What ecclesiastical systems cannot accomplish, the simple act of faith can achieve in the life of the individual who looks to the crucified and risen Lord.

In organized churches around the world are to be found individuals who somehow trust in the organization to effect salvation for them. Prestige seems to accumulate through centuries of continued existence, and a sense of security is frequently derived from the claim that one's church has stood through many changing centuries. The typical error of regular church attenders is to rely upon the contact of that church for their salvation.

Much variety is to be found when individuals are asked to relate their experiences. The most startling discovery they make is when they finally place their entire trust in the merit of the risen Saviour. Then they realize that it is not the church that saves at all, but that only Christ can save. Anastasia made that discovery when she was walking through Central Park on a Sunday afternoon when Billy Graham preached the Gospel from the Band Shell.

She was the daughter of Russian parents, and from earliest childhood had a hatred of all who were converted away from the Russian Orthodox Church. This church, she had been taught, was the oldest of all, and others had broken away from its fellowship. She had known many Baptists in Russia, and hated them especially for their zeal in making converts. She did see in them however a people who studied the Scriptures. She had been raised on the catechism only.

In America, she continued attendance in the Orthodox Russian Church. Church going, however, became spasmodic and rare after a while. When Anastasia was married, it was by a Justice of the Peace. This later seemed strange and wrong to her and to her husband, for they began regular church attendance almost at once. For ten years they continued in her church, and she loved the church and its impressive ritual.

She said, "I often thought of God when going to Mass. The priest would preach a sermon from the Bible, but it left me unchanged. My interest grew and I studied the Sunday school literature and history of our church. I would read about the martyrs and wonder if I would be willing to die for the church as they did. I did not feel that I would be willing to do so. Even so, many people thought of me as a good Christian, and I considered myself one.

"I even thought I was a better Christian than those members of other churches that were not orthodox as mine.

"I am an assistant buyer in one of the large chain stores. When the Billy Graham meeting started, two of the girls in the office kept asking me to go with them to the Crusade. I kept making excuses when really I could have gone. I was against such a thing, and at the same time I knew that my church had not given me all that I needed. I was really spiritually hungry. I decided to go hear Billy personally after watching him on television one night. The next day he was to preach at Central Park, and I went to hear him. I decided not to hear him again because he made me so angry.

"I was supposed to go with a lady to the Garden the next night, but when I tried to excuse myself, she felt hurt. I decided to go with her. I made my decision that night after talking with a counselor for more than an hour. The next day I was so angry with Billy—I knew I would have to leave my church. I loved my church and wept bitterly at the thought of leaving it. It was the church of my parents and of my grandparents. I always thought its ceremony was beautiful and impressive. I didn't want to leave it, and I was blaming Billy for all this.

"Because of this bitterness, I refused to attend the meetings. I went to the Christian life classes that met nightly before the main service, but I said to myself that Billy Graham was not important. I didn't have to listen to him. I wasn't converted to a man. This feeling did not continue for long, because I soon could see that I was foolish putting the blame on anyone. I decided to go back to hear him. I went almost every night after that. Now that the Crusade is over, I have found and joined a very active Baptist church. I am still amazed at what I have done because I had always hated Baptists from the time I heard of them leaving the church in Russia.

"I like this church because the preacher is a teacher of the Bible. I take notes all the time he is speaking. God has so wonderfully helped me. I used to think I must have a drink every night after work, but God has taken the desire away. I never thought I could get along without it,

but it has been easy. I was a regular movie-goer, and I
remember how shocked I was when a woman in the Bible
class I attend said something against it. I spoke out saying
that I didn't want to be *that* holy. I did attend a movie a
few days later. I had never before noticed all the vulgarity
and sin portrayed in them. I got up and walked out, and
haven't been to see one since that night. Now I don't have
time, because I go to my Bible class and prayer meeting.
In fact, I never before knew what church people did when
they didn't partake in some of the things of the world, but
I have enjoyed the busiest months of my life since I was
converted.

"This experience has opened up to me a world I hadn't
known since childhood. I'm learning to read the Bible,
something I've always wanted to do. I find indecision,
self-consciousness, doubt, and all the little annoyances
fall away and leave me free to live every day most peace-
fully. I know now why the martyrs through the ages were
willing to die for Christ, and I know too that I would be
willing should the world situation come to that again."

Anastasia told her story with tears. In Russia she knew
relatives who were still spiritually bound and blind. She
wondered if some day Billy Graham might go to her
people to bring them the knowledge of salvation. She
asked that many would pray that the message might
reach the millions in Russia and enlighten those who were
still in the same darkness that she had experienced for
so long.

Back in her office today she sheds the light of the Gospel
to all who are associated with her. The complete trans-

formation that has taken place in her life is evidence of the verse found in Romans 1:16: "For I am not ashamed of the gospel of Christ: for it is the power of God unto salvation to every one that believeth; to the Jew first, and also to the Greek."

6. Business with God

WALL STREET is without doubt one of the best known streets in the world, at least by name. It has become the symbol of big business and the American philosophy of free enterprise and competition. This much-criticized phase of the American way is still one that is open to all, and thousands of small investors watch with great interest and concern the rise and fall of the stock market. In this part of New York are to be found thousands of men and women engaged in high finance. These persons have often been thought of as lacking in spiritual concern or insight. Nevertheless, one of the satisfactions received during the Crusade was the knowledge that many of them had for years recognized the deceitfulness of riches and had sought for treasures where moth and rust do not corrupt and where thieves do not break through nor steal.

J.T. was one of these. From his desk on the sixteenth floor of one of the largest brokerage offices in the world, he could sense the pulse of the financial affairs of big and small business alike. He had come to know the panic and fear of thousands when the market would drop a fraction and the thrill when it would rise. All around him were busy secretaries, and machines that were literally hot from running at high speed, to record every change in the value of numberless corporation securities as well as in the uncertain whims of people whose life savings were invested in industry and business.

J.T. was well known throughout all the offices that occupied the entire building, one of the largest in the Wall Street section of Manhattan. While seated in a comfortable dining room in the basement of the building, he told the story of his life and of experiences that finally resulted in his salvation. His father had spent his life in the same business. He had been a man of honest business principles, yet religiously he was a skeptic. J.T.'s mother was somewhat more religious and encouraged attendance at Sunday school.

"I always considered myself a Christian," he said, "because I had been baptized in the church. I always went to Sunday school, even though I didn't attend the church service very often. I didn't understand what the preacher was trying to get across. I didn't continue in any one denomination, but changed four or five times. If association with the church can save, I certainly should be saved. My religion was more one of doing good than one of holding any particular doctrines. I didn't think they were important. Often I went out of my way to help people and do acts of kindness. Now that I think of it, it was because it gave me a kind of personal satisfaction and standing. I realize that even my righteous acts, as the Bible says, were like filthy rags. Then I didn't see it quite that way, but I do now."

J.T. was then asked if there might have been any particular event that stimulated his thinking on the spiritual side of things. The only one he could think of was a keen disappointment in a girl friend he had been going with. "We had been going together for some time, and had considered marriage. She even went to the same church I did, and was one of the Sunday school teachers. But I don't recall that we ever discussed Christ. She is still teaching there. What upset me completely for a time was that she started to go out with another fellow, and before long we broke up. That was some time ago. I don't think that during this crisis in my life I ever thought about God or my own spiritual need.

"Shortly after this affair, I remember the Billy Graham Crusade was on in London. Of course the press carried reports on the meeting there, and like most people, I read about it with great interest. I think that what made the greatest impression on me then was the fact that the British would receive an American with such enthusiasm.

"In the intervening years I didn't think much more about Billy Graham or the Gospel he was preaching, but when I found that he was coming to New York, my sister and I thought of going to hear him.

"When the meetings did finally start, however, we both

kept making excuses. I remember one night I had a
meeting to attend and my sister was going to a sewing
club. Finally at the last minute we both just forgot these
engagements and went to hear Billy.

"I don't really remember much about the first sermon
I heard. I just remember that as I sat there I found myself
literally hanging on to the chair. I can't explain why,
because I really wasn't aware of any conflict at that time.
The next night we went again. That night Billy preached
on the heart. He said that the Bible taught that it was
wicked and deceitful. It was a strange idea to me, because to just about everyone else I seemed good. To make
a confession of sin and need somehow didn't seem to be
the thing to do. But down in my heart I knew I was lost.
I did not have nearly the emotion that second night that
I did on the first. I just felt that I was there in the Garden
alone with God. This was an unusual thing for me, because I am always conscious of the presence of people,
and especially a crowd. This night it was different. I
didn't have to be good to show people I was good. I was
there before God, and for the first time I realized how
sinful I was.

"I went forward as others were doing, though even
then I felt so alone. Other people made no impression
on me. I was making a decision I believed I must make
whether any other person did or not. As we went down
to the counseling room, a young fellow joined me and
pointed out from the Scriptures just how one may know
that he is saved. I was quite confused right then. I thought
he used too much Scripture, but then I had to admit that

through it God spoke to my heart. From that moment on my life has been entirely different.

"It wasn't necessary for me to change jobs. My work was a perfectly ethical and useful work. I was so changed, though, that one person after another mentioned it. From that night on I have been really walking on air. I used to worry a great deal, but now I just have no problems. It's a wonderful thing. I don't suppose it goes that way with every person who comes forward, but that is what God did in my life.

"It's wonderful how the Lord gives you something to do. For me, it seems that I am to accept civic responsibility. For example, I have volunteered to assist in setting up the new procedure for registration. It is a service someone must do for the community and for the country. I believe that I must do this as my responsibility as a Christian. I think that we should get in and make Christ known to people this way.

"At first it was difficult to get into a church. I went around a little and found that some preachers were really preaching the Gospel while others were philosophizing. I think that all of those who, like myself, were converted at the Crusade are looking for a clear presentation of the Gospel. Until all of us have found such a church home, we have organized a group of young business and professional men to meet together on Monday nights to study the Bible. What we all want, mainly, is to get some good Bible study. It was through the Bible that we first came to Christ and we now have a desire to know the whole Bible as well as we can."

It is characteristic of most Crusades that men and women, young and old, all stand together somewhere at the front of an auditorium or field to declare publicly their desire to trust Christ and Him alone for salvation. As an observer watches them find their way, there is no way of knowing their inner thoughts and the train of circumstances that has finally brought them to a decision for Christ.

On a particular night in the spring of 1954, there stood a distinguished gentleman surrounded by hundreds who were making the same decision he had come to make. Nearly four years after that night, Charles told the story so that others might be encouraged to make the same commitment to Christ. He was one of those persons who grow up in the midst of religious people, but is untouched by their profession. He could remember only that upon the few occasions he had attended the church, he had heard no clear Gospel message. He had been baptized and confirmed and assumed that such ordinances make one a Christian, though he could not explain why.

Charles had inherited a prosperous food-processing business, and by his careful and wise management it had become a major industry in one of the quaint English towns some miles from London. Unfortunately, he became addicted to drink and had actually come to jeopardize the business because of drunkenness. He became a confirmed alcoholic, though he never intended to do so. Again and again he was warned by his associates, and finally threatened by them. He was in danger of losing all he owned through alcohol. In such a condition, anyone would have thought that he was in need of some radical change. Being a man of exceptional determination, he resolved never to touch liquor again. Weeks slipped by and then months. Charles did not drink. Once more he gave active direction to a business that had slumped, and brought it back to solvency. He was more than a success now.

This resolution and his victory over liquor had its accompanying evils. Now he became very proud of the achievement, and very hard to get along with. He quarreled with his wife at home and with the men in the processing plant. One of the men who worked with him was an active Christian. He urged Charles to plan a caravan of busses to take the workers in a body to hear the American evangelist, Billy Graham, who was then in meetings in London.

Charles was agreeable, but thought it best first to visit and observe himself. He wanted to be sure that it was something fit for his workers. His wife, who knew more about the Crusade than he, had made him promise not to go forward.

He recalled, "I was deeply impressed with the fact that Billy knew Jesus. His frequent expression, 'The Bible says,' made me realize that I had a conflict with God, not Graham. As I listened, I realized how much I was in need. I had not had a drink for more than two years, but I lived in constant dread of a relapse. I knew I was still a target of the devil of drink. I remembered a time when I was in Ireland on business and how I was sorely tempted. All of this made me realize that the moral resolu-

tion had not changed me but had just suspended some of
my worst practices.

"As Billy continued to preach, he began to bear down
on the sins of the spirit, and at this point I was as guilty
as anyone. My pride still kept me from making any decision. After a while Billy said, 'If Jesus carried the cross
all the way to Calvary for you, you can trust Him with all
that you have.' I felt that that statement was inspired,
for it struck me and went right into my very soul. I
couldn't resist from then on. I didn't know much about
Billy's religion yet, for it was the first night I had been
there, and I had never heard anyone like him in my life.
But he challenged me to trust Jesus with everything I had.
I went forward with the rest, forgetting my pride, and
hoping for mercy from God.

"I was terrified as I went into the counseling room. The
young man who counseled me wouldn't let me go, once
we got there. After showing me some verses, he began
praying for me. He prayed so earnestly I was unable to
resist. I somehow felt that God must answer his prayer.
I was relieved, and my burden was gone. I couldn't help
wondering what the next day would be like, but as I
awakened the next morning, I said, 'Thank you God,' for
I knew the miraculous change had taken place. I was a
new person. God had saved me forever for Jesus' sake.

"The counselor had given me a verse the night before.
It said, 'There hath no temptation taken you but such as
is common to man: but God is faithful, who will not suffer
you to be tempted above that ye are able; but will with the
temptation also make a way to escape, that ye may be

able to bear it.' I have experienced this many times. I know today God is faithful."

A few days after his remarkable conversion, Charles desired some way to show his great appreciation to Billy Graham. He rented one of the largest theaters in the city of London, and advertised a great rally where Billy might bring the Gospel to many who had not come to Harringay. That warmth has continued without abating until the present time. This summer, during the New York Crusade, Charles came from London to receive the blessing of the New York Crusade. When he was asked to make a comparison between the two meetings, he replied, "This is another Harringay. It's just like going back four years and living it over again. The only difference is, today I am a Christian watching others come to the Saviour who so wonderfully met my need that night in London."

Dave is one who knows the meaning of beginning all over again. He was one of the young executives who might be seen almost any day rushing along Madison Avenue and turning in to one of the many offices of the advertising agencies. He was an account executive, and according to any standard he would have been judged to be more than average. A very young man, he had already gone to the top in his field. Financially he was secure.

But Dave was like many other young and aggressive executives in the city who cover their deep-seated sense of need with an exterior of self-sufficiency. As he went in and out of the office day after day, he gave the impression of one who had every ambition fulfilled according to schedule. But there was a whole area of Dave's life that demanded satisfaction. He was spiritually hungry without knowing what the problem was.

"All my life I have resisted any religious influence, and at times have made fun of it," he related, "for my mother was a believer, and my father came from a very strict background and was a very strict person himself. Religion was very distasteful to me because it seemed that it took away from you much more than it gave. I was made to go to Sunday school until I was in the ninth grade, and then I lost interest. They didn't give a very good Bible training in our Sunday school. I can remember that it consisted mainly of pleasant stories, poorly told. They gave the impression in our Sunday school that Jesus was a nice man, but never did they teach that He was God who was able to save.

"So you see, my growing years did not happen to be years of spiritual training or development. I was as much without God as if I had been born in a pagan country where nobody knows anything about the Bible. I never thought much about God except when I was in college, and then He was merely a subject for academic speculation. I remember slightly the William James theory of God, and I think I accepted that theory as much as any. It seemed to me that men believed in God because they needed to, and not because there actually was a God.

"My college career was interrupted by a call to military service. I was in the Coast Guard for a time and then returned to resume my studies. I was studying television production at Michigan. When my college work was done I returned to the armed services for another stretch. I was sure of myself, and thought I could get along on my own. This time in the army I went to the bad morally. When I became completely disgusted with myself, I went to the base chapel to confer with the chaplain. From him I received no help at all. I did meet some fine chaplains during my days in the army, but the time I needed one the most, I got no help. I needed the message of the Bible, though I didn't realize it then.

"When I at last reached a place where standards were totally gone and where I was headed for destruction, I remember I made a promise to God that I would mend my ways. I didn't have an understanding of God then, but He must have known that my desire was for good. I had gotten tired of sitting in bars and taverns all the time. That didn't seem to be the life for a man. So I turned to intellectual pursuits. Reading became a hobby and I began to develop my mind. I adopted a standard for conduct and tried to hold to it.

"Although my home was in Detroit, after I got out of the army I came to New York. I had a desire to break into big business. I had been on the staff of the university television as a camera producer, but that seemed to lack the big-time challenge I wanted. I had been having a real battle with my language for one thing. All the time I was in the army I was so profane that when I came back to civilian life I felt I must learn a new language. After some additional schooling, I broke into the advertising business.

"About the time I was just getting into 'big business,'

Billy Graham announced the New York Crusade. I had
heard of him when he was in London, but after that I
had forgotten about the work he was doing. What religion I had was not connected with the church, but it was
rather a kind of rationalistic religion. When I planned to
go to hear him, it was not because I had a spiritual concern, but I just thought he should be heard. The little
spiritual concern I had when I was in the army had passed
over and I no longer had a sense of need.

"I had to stand in line for a while at Madison Square
Garden to get in, and I remember I made some wise remarks about religion and about Billy, as my roommate and
I stood there. I really think it was a cover up, because I
knew he might preach right straight at me. We both
finally found a seat and listened to the service. At first I
just looked on it as a super job of showmanship. Everything was so well done and well planned. The choir was
larger than any I had ever seen. I was really quite impressed. However, it was much more like church than I
had anticipated. There was a quiet reverence all around,
and I even began to feel reverent myself.

"Then Billy began to do just what I had heard he did.
He began to give verses from the Bible on his subject. I
think what impressed me most was the simplicity with
which he spoke. The churches I had attended just didn't
tell how to know God. I think they assumed that because
we were educated, we knew something about religion.
Actually I was ignorant. I had never heard anything about
the new birth or faith. That was just what Billy talked
about. He hadn't been speaking long before I had quite

forgotten my skeptical attitude. The wise remarks I had made certainly didn't apply in any way to what was taking place in that building.

"When the invitation was extended, I turned to my roommate and told him of my desire to go forward. That must have surprised him, because he had been more interested in coming to the meeting than I had. He refused, when I told him I was going. It was a very definite thing so far as I was concerned. I had thought that these people who go forward must move on their emotions. Perhaps some of them do, but I knew clearly what I went for. I should add, however, that several days later, when it was clear that a great change had come, I did actually have some emotion about it. In fact, right now when I consider what Christ has done for me, and how long I resisted, I become emotional.

"This decision has meant a great deal to me. In fact, it has had the effect of completely turning my life around. My roommate has been doing a lot of kidding about it, and the men in the office can't understand what has happened. They notice it when I no longer take a drink with them. I don't even smoke, whereas I was formerly a chain-smoker. In fact, there are certain things in my present business that I cannot continue doing, and my business depends upon doing them."

The sequel to Dave's story is that he is no longer in the advertising business. So strong were some of his convictions concerning some practices, that he felt God directing him into another field of activity. Dave is back in Detroit. After he decided to make a change of occupation, an offer came to him to produce an educational television program. This is an experimental kind of educational procedure sponsored by the university. Here Dave felt he could render a service that would be in keeping with his former training, but more especially with his recent profession of personal faith in Jesus Christ.

Every individual must make decisions appropriate to his own conscience as the Word of God sheds light on the problems of the day. The clear evidence that God has wrought a change in this man's heart is his willingness to follow the leading God gives concerning the whole of his life. This is the ultimate test of the genuineness of one's faith.

"All my life I have been associated with the church." This statement is familiar to any who listen to the story of those who have had a personal encounter with Christ. If any one thing is true, it is that it is not the church alone in any of its branches that can save, but only Christ who can deliver a soul from the guilt and penalty of sin. The opening quotation is a statement made by Tom, a young salesman. It was not an indication of an antagonistic attitude nor of intellectual dullness.

At the age of twenty-six, Tom had the ability to sell his product and had already made a success of his career. His ambition and pleasant personality combined to make him tops in his field.

Tom had always been around the church, for his parents were church people. While still in high school, and through his college years, he taught a Sunday school class of young fellows. In high school he had been a member of the youth fellowship. But through these years, Tom admitted, "I never opened the Bible." When he was asked about what was taught in the Sunday school class, he confessed that if he ever touched upon the lesson, it was not more than to read a bit from the quarterly magazine.

Tom said, "Like many persons who are active in religious work, I just thought I was a Christian. I really didn't know what the word meant. To me the matter of being a Christian was to follow a certain ethical pattern. I can see now that it isn't possible to do it that way. You have to have some power to overcome temptation and to keep you from slipping into sins of all kinds."

Tom was no different from any average young man growing up. He liked girls and liquor. "Some of the girls I went with mere 'character girls,' and I can't figure out why I got such a kick out of going with them. They were mostly 'blind dates' I had during college. It's a funny thing, but I was afraid I wouldn't get married. In fact, up until the time of the Crusade I was running after first one girl and then another. As far as drinking went, I didn't exactly become a drunkard. In fact, I seldom drank that much, but it was enough so that our social functions got pretty wild. They didn't seem that way at the time, but since I have come to Christ, I realize how off-color they were.

"I had another problem that showed up during my time in college. I was studying to be a coach. I had such a violent temper that after flying off the handle a few times,

I was dismissed from college. I never did finish, not on account of my grades, but on account of my uncontrollable temper. When they dropped me from college, it was time to do my stretch in the army. I spent two years in Europe as one of Uncle Sam's defenders. It was while I was in the army that I did have a time of spiritual concern. Getting away from home and from things that gave me the feeling of belonging to something left me empty and afraid. I began going to chapel on the base, but it was little help. I went to the chaplain about my drinking one time, and all he did was to show me it wasn't so bad. He tried to convince me that it was just a soldier's way of getting away from the grind and routine of hard army life. Although I wasn't then a Christian, I knew his advice had missed the mark. I expected he would tell me how to win in the battle with my habits. Instead he just said that it was a battle you couldn't win, so why try. You can see that I was at least making a good try every once in a while, but I never did hear the Gospel preached directly at me as Billy did last summer.

"When the Crusade was about to begin, I was asked to be a counselor. I didn't know what that meant really. Out of curiosity I said I'd do it because I wanted to see what they did in one of those meetings. I had only attended one or two of the instruction classes when I knew that I wouldn't make a counselor. Charlie Riggs was our teacher, and he kept saying that to be a good counselor a person must know that he is saved. I had never heard much about being saved. I never knew that you could know you were saved. I didn't believe that was possible. The result was that after just a meeting or two, I was so mixed up that I decided to drop out. It was too much Bible for me. I had thought counseling was just giving practical advice, such as we studied in a counseling class in college, but Charlie meant that it was to be able to find in the Bible the answers to the questions the inquirers would ask.

"Finally I went to one of the team members, Gene Soderberg. I told him of my intentions to drop out, and he said I might just stay around and help distribute papers and do such things. I thought he was so considerate about it that I agreed to stay. That was what kept me coming for many weeks." Through the four months of the Crusade, Tom could be seen serving as an usher or rendering some important service to the people who came to hear the message of the Gospel.

"You see," he continued, "I didn't really make my decision as some of the people did. I met many who responded to the invitation the first or second time they heard the message. I heard Billy preach over and over again. I was very slow about making the decision, and even when it seemed that it was the only right thing to do, I still resisted. It was a hard thing for me to admit that as a Sunday school teacher and church worker, I hadn't even been a Christian. I would have to face my Sunday school class and the people in the church and admit that I had been a fraud all the time. That was too much for me, because I was proud of my religious activity and influence with the youth in our church.

"From the start of the Crusade, I knew something was lacking in my life. I had gone to church because it was a good place to contact people. I was sociable and enjoyed such activity. I was afraid I was going to the Crusade for the same reason, and felt I was just being a hypocrite. It's a strange thing how I finally came to make definite the decision. I recall that on a certain Saturday night Billy was preaching on the problems of the home and family. I was listening carefully. I had a date that night, but I was certain she was the wrong girl for me. After a while, Billy spoke directly to me when he said that God had the right girl for every young fellow and the right fellow for the girl. It took just that to make me see I wasn't trusting the Lord. I learned in that statement what it meant to trust Him, not just for some things in life, but for everything.

"My feelings were very mixed. I knew he was right when he was speaking about such things, but it made me angry to have him call me a sinner. I knew I was a sinner, but who was he to call me one? I still resisted his preaching. Even my mother had said she hoped I wouldn't get involved in this business. But my time had come. That night I felt I couldn't just go on as I had been. Billy said that there are some decisions which, if *you* don't make them now, time will make them for you. I knew he was right, and in a moment I stood and was on my way, not caring any longer what anyone thought.

"Down in the counseling room, a young salesman came to talk with me. In this coincidence I could already see that the Lord was ahead of me, planning things. This fellow could speak my language, and yet he knew the Lord and he knew the Bible. I didn't know just how it would work, and I was afraid that the next day I would be just the same as I had always been. I couldn't believe that such a change would actually take place and make me have new thoughts and desires. But the next day, I knew that a great thing had happened to me. I *was* born again.

"That was the best thing that ever happened to me. I'm never alone any more, and I always know that there is One who is interested in me and who cares. I have a new attitude on the job. I'm not trying to beat the other salesmen any more, but I'm trying to do my best so everyone can see what Christ has done for me. I'm not incomplete any more, nor am I in competition at work. In fact, through the summer, I refused to attend some of the sales meetings so I could be at the Crusade meetings. I lost a very important promotion by not being there. Since then the Lord has been helping me, and I'm sure I didn't lose anything that can compare with what I have gained."

Jesus once asked the question, "For what shall it profit a man, if he shall gain the whole world, and lose his own soul? Or what shall a man give in exchange for his soul?" Tom had come to the place where he knew that no gain would ever compensate for the spiritual riches that are received through that act of decisive faith. When he said, "It's the best thing that ever happened to me," he expressed a deep conviction that is characteristic of all who lay down their burden of sin at the cross and receive eternal life through the merit of the blood of Jesus Christ.

Today, Tom is a changed person. Nearly half a year has elapsed since he first felt the solid influence of the message of Christ. Now he recalls the years of frustration and self-condemnation, the moments of depression and flight from reality. Today, like multitudes, he has a buoyant faith that has given him happiness and joy. Life is at last worth living. This young man who was once dead in trespasses and sins, is now alive through faith in Jesus Christ.

7. *The Great Physician*

BOBBI IS AN INSTRUCTOR of nurses in one of the Metropolitan hospitals. Her red hair is appropriate to her disposition, and she is youthful in appearance and attitude. After a busy day instructing nurses, she came across the city to the Billy Graham Crusade office to tell the story of her life and the events that finally brought her to know the Great Physician.

Germany was the place of her birth, but in Holland she grew to young womanhood. Her Jewish mother forgot her original religion when she married Bobbi's Lutheran father. Neither of them made any attempt to direct Bobbi in the way that leads to life everlasting. They had been driven from the fatherland in the days of Hitler and Naziism because of her mother's Jewish ancestry. But even in Holland, when the bombs were reducing one city after another to rubble and soldiers marched through the débris-ridden streets, Bobbi had no thought of God.

She said, "I had a German Bible but never read it. It was given to me as a gift, and like many people, I used it as a safe place to press flowers and keep letters or small notes from friends. I thought all religions were ridiculous. I had been to church with some friends. I remember standing towards the back of the big church behind one of the huge pillars and laughing at what went on. When they took an offering, I refused to give anything. When any of my friends talked about God, as they sometimes did, I would laugh at them or be annoyed.

"After coming to America I never went to church. My excuse was that I couldn't understand the language well enough. I had trained for nursing in Holland and thought I could nurse when I came here, but I had to take some training here before I could. Finally I got a position in a hospital, and now I am teaching trainees.

"One day one of the nurses came to me and asked me to go with her to hear Billy Graham. She was a very friendly Norwegian girl, and because I liked her so much I agreed to go before I really thought about it. I found out later what it was and was sorry I had promised. I just didn't want to go to any religious meeting. As far as Billy Graham was concerned, I had never heard of him. I don't know how I had missed him, because he was in Holland at the time I was there. I found that out later.

"The night we went to the meeting I was very antagonistic. I must have been a poor companion for the girl who invited me. Now I know that she asked me because she sensed that I needed salvation. I don't remember much about the sermon except one thing. Billy Graham said that you must believe or you are not saved. I thought to myself, 'Saved for what?' I just didn't know what he meant when he said saved. Then I found my mind wandering. I looked all around at the crowd and wished I had not come. We went home after the meeting, and all I could think was that it had been a wasted evening.

"All the next day I kept thinking about the talk I had heard about being saved, and it bothered me. I wasn't so concerned except I didn't know what it meant and I didn't want to ask anyone. So the next night I decided to go alone. I wanted to think about it without being noticed. I didn't want to admit that I knew so little about religion. I went forward that night to receive help. When I got down in the counseling room the girl showed me some verses. She was very helpful. She asked me to pray. I had never prayed before in my life, and I just couldn't pray. I was so ashamed, I got up and rushed out.

"I went the next two nights, and both nights I went alone for the same reason. The third night they must have recognized me, because Mrs. Piat was my counselor that night. She is the wife of a team member. She was so helpful to me, and she could speak Dutch, which made me feel good. After this third time I was satisfied. I suppose some people think it strange, but I knew so little about it that I needed to hear it over and over. Finally the Lord made it clear to me and I was saved for sure.

"It was the Word of God that convinced me of my sin and need. I thank God that I came to know of this wonderful way. I know that I have been saved because even the nurses who are my students can see the difference. Before I took Jesus as my Saviour, when they would make mistakes, I would scream at them in anger. I don't do that any more. A few days after my conversion I went to them and begged their forgiveness for my past ways and bad temper. Another thing I notice is that I'm not nervous any more as I used to be.

"Before that night when I was converted, I used to be very bored with life. Now, thank God, I am so happy. There was a time when I thought Bible reading was foolish, but now I can't read enough. It is like bread to my soul that I need every day. I had never gone to church, but since that day I have been going regularly. I remember the first one I went to after I found the Lord. The members were dancing. I had thought it would be a Bible study meeting. I never went to that one again, but I have found one where the true Word of God is preached. Surely I have much to thank God for. I had to come to America and to New York before I could find salvation, but I have found it in Christ finally. Nursing used to be my duty and my profession. Now I enjoy it because I can help people. I hope now I will be able to give them the spiritual healing as well as to care for their bodies."

Billy Graham is not the only evangelist who has preached that conversion is instantaneous. The major evangelists all held that a man is born again the moment he receives Christ as Saviour from sin. Students of the phenomena of conversion have observed that certain individuals find difficulty in defining the exact moment when the decision was made. Many dedicated believers cannot be certain as to the precise moment when Christ came in saving power and transformed them, but it is believed that their inability to do so is because they were not at the time able to reflect and observe. The absence of high emotion at this time is the most usual reason for being unable to look back to *one* big moment.

Those converted in their more mature years can almost without exception point to a moment of decision. Beth said, "The change was instantaneous." She was twenty-two at the time, and found no difficulty in recalling the events that led up to her conversion. She had lived in the vicinity of London from her birth and had attended Sunday school. She had never had Bible teaching, for her parents were nothing more than nominal Christians, and she attended Sunday school only while very young.

Like many others, when she was asked whether she considered herself a Christian, she answered, "I never gave it a thought. My mother died when I was yet very young, and for a while I went to church, but nothing I heard seemed to have anything to do with my personal problems. The only reason I went to church at all was that I was afraid I might miss something. I couldn't get over the sorrow caused by my mother's death. More than once I was on the verge of a breakdown, and I believed it was on account of my sorrow.

"I trained for nursing when I became old enough. I always wanted to help people who were in trouble. But I must have appeared to be very sad during the years I worked with those who so much needed cheer. In fact after I had been converted, many of my fellow nurses remarked about how happy I seemed.

"When Billy Graham came to London, some of the nurses in the hospital were planning to go in a delegation to the Harringay Arena. When they asked me, I said I didn't care to go. I didn't want to admit my ignorance, but I didn't know what an evangelist was. One by one, the nurses backed out, having other commitments the night they had planned to go. I remember one of them came rushing up to me and explained how she couldn't go. She handed me a ticket for that very night and said to me, 'You go in my place.' Strangely, I just thought I'd have to go since I had the ticket, and she couldn't go.

"It never occurred to me that I might be converted that night. I had been morally clean all my life. My sins were more the sins of omission, and they hadn't condemned me at all. I listened to Billy as he preached, and I was quite surprised. I had expected to see something much more dramatic, but he was very conservative. The whole service was filled with a feeling of reverence. I can't remember the sermon now after four years, but I distinctly remember the effect the invitation had upon me. He held out his arms as he customarily does, and simply said, 'Come and receive Christ.' I was stunned, as if something had struck me. Actually no one spoke a word to me, but I immediately went forward with others and then went on to the counseling room. I did not receive much help there, perhaps because I was so shaken over what I had done. There was

a male nurse there who did help me, but all I remember
is that he showed me the verse that says, 'For God so loved
the world, that he gave his only begotten Son, that whosoever believeth in him should not perish, but have everlasting life.' I know the verse well now, but I believe I
had not heard it before that night. He emphasized that
God's love was for the world, but that the word 'whosoever' meant that the individual must believe in order
to be saved.

"Even though I didn't know exactly what I had done, I
found that I was very calm within, whereas I had been
very troubled right until the minute I answered the call
that Billy extended that night. I was no longer miserable,
but had a deep peace in my heart and mind.

"The test came the next day. Except for the fact that I
had such a peace in my soul, I couldn't notice any other
evidence. I knew I was trusting in Christ for my salvation,
but I did not yet know what the new birth was. I have
learned so much from the Bible since then that I can look
back and tell all that was taking place in my heart. At any
rate, I went to my job as usual. But as I went among the
sick people in my ward, and also as I came in contact with
other nurses, they began to make comments. I hadn't told
a soul of my going to Harringay or to the Crusade. Above
all, I didn't mention my going forward because I was still
stunned and amazed at myself.

"I listened to remarks made through the day, and one
of the nurses said, 'Beth, you look so happy today. You
never used to smile. I'm so glad for you.' I finally explained
as best I could what had happened. They could scarcely

believe that a person could change so suddenly. But I know that it is possible. It was some time before I was able to comprehend it, and even now I sometimes return in thought to that night and wonder at the goodness of God in saving me.

"About a fortnight after I had received Christ, I finally called my aunt. I usually called her more frequently and she wondered why I had not called. I explained that I felt that I must be certain before I told her, but that now I was confident that a great and lasting change had come. The great sorrow over my mother's death had changed. I still felt the loss of a mother, but Christ had filled that aching void I had felt for so long.

"That was four years ago. Coming here to the New York Crusade has been such a blessing to me. It was almost like going back to Harringay and living it all over again. This has been the most wonderful experience since then, for my faith has been immeasurably strengthened. But even had I not been able to visit this Crusade, and see some of the friends who helped me so much, I would have gone on with Christ anyhow, for He has become a constant friend to me."

8. Treadmill of Oblivion

ONLY GOD KNOWS how many office girls are on the "tread-mill of oblivion." This expression is the way one of them described the endless, boring routine of their daily life. Every morning they dart down into the subway to emerge somewhere on the island of Manhattan to begin the day's grind in an office. They don't even have enough money to be able to eat medium-priced meals. It's either a sand-wich they have wrapped up and carried in a coat pocket, or a run-out to Woolworth's for the forty-five-cent special lunch, or a hot dog at Nedick's. By quitting time, they haven't enough energy for more exciting activity than an occasional movie. The biggest problem is: where can you meet eligible young men in the big city?

Eventually every one of these office girls feels the gnaw-ing loneliness that causes her to do strange things. Some seek to drown their feelings in superficial amusements. A very small number seek for some comfort in religion. Many of them came to the Crusade, not necessarily to seek the Lord, but it was something to do, something everyone was talking about. A visit would fill up an eve-ning and give them much to talk about later.

The stories of these working girls are alike and yet different. There is the same loneliness, the same feeling of futility, the sense of guilt when some sin is indulged in to relieve the horrible monotony of it all. Yet in nearly every instance there is the desire for a sense of security and belonging to someone. Self-righteous persons have condemned the wayward girl without knowing that many times her pursuit of the basic satisfactions of life had become distorted and perverted.

Those who have not observed the wonderful transformation that takes place in the life that turns to Christ for pardon are not aware of the sufficiency of Christ, but in the frequently-told story of conversion there is the familiar expression of His adequacy for every human need. Those who told their stories concur in saying that they now have a sense of completeness in their trust in Christ. He has met their need and has exceeded their asking.

Ruth was one of those who could look back upon her life before it became Christ's, and recall the many unsatisfied desires. Although her parents had at some time in the past manifested a vital interest in the things of the spirit, they had gone so far back that if there had ever been a vital faith in Christ, it could not now be recognized. They had continued to frequent the church long after the warm and vital faith had degenerated into cold formality. Ruth herself sought for satisfaction in the church of her parents. It seemed to promise so much that the world could not offer, but though she remained within the organization of the church, she never could draw from the mechanics of religion the water of life. Her active participation in youth groups and membership in the choir did not provide an adequate challenge nor did it put a song in her heart. Even when she was ordained a deaconess in the church, there was no motivating faith that sent her forth to minister in the things of Christ.

Still, Ruth was very self-satisfied. Her religious activity did provide a sense of righteousness that immunized her to the true Gospel. When she finally came to the Crusade, it was more to be amused than to receive spiritual enlightenment. She told her own story more beautifully than another could possibly tell it, in a letter of appreciation in which she related her experience. She affirmed it all in a later interview. Here are her own words:

"Prior to May 21, 1957, if anyone had told me that I would be writing a letter on what the Billy Graham Crusade has meant to me, I would have suggested they see a good psychiatrist.

"My church had arranged to have two hundred tickets for the meeting at Madison Square Garden on May 21 and I decided to go along and see the show. I had no use for evangelists (never having seen one, I considered myself an authority), and I pictured them as characters tearing at their hair and sending everyone to eternal damnation. I felt I certainly didn't need to go—I was a good Christian and had been to church all my life. I had grown up in the Sunday school and the young people's organizations. In fact, in January I was ordained as a deaconess of the church.

"On the evening of May 21, 1957, all of these smug, self-satisfied ideas were certainly changed. That night Dr.

Graham was speaking on the Ten Commandments. He spoke on prayer, reading the Bible, and most important of all, on having a personal friendship with the Lord. I don't think I have ever been so humbled or so shamed before in my life. The realization came to me that church membership wasn't enough. For a long time I had felt the lack of direction, the lack of something really solid in my life, but not knowing what this lack was, I suppressed these feelings by devoting myself to the organizations of the church. Through Dr. Graham's sermon that evening I realized how completely I had been neglecting my Lord. I had been utterly ignoring the Saviour who had hung on the cross in my place, for my sins. I had never seriously considered the fact that I had sinned, in fact, I had once half-jokingly and half-seriously told a clergyman that I didn't consider myself a sinner at all.

"Before I met the Lord, prayer was something that took a few minutes before bedtime, if I managed to stay awake long enough. Bible reading was something I had always been going to do but somehow never seemed to find the time for; and as far as personal encounter with Jesus Christ was concerned, I frankly didn't know what Mr. Graham was talking about.

"I went home that first night deeply disturbed. I had wanted to go forward but didn't because my pride wouldn't let me. So many of my friends were present at the Garden that night and in my imagination I could hear their choice comments to me if I had made a decision. The next night, May 22, I joined the Crusade choir. That evening I was again aware of how dreadfully short I had fallen of the glory of God. When the invitation came, however, I again allowed my pride to hold me back. I knew the price of accepting Christ was high and I didn't know if I was willing to pay it.

"Friday, May 24, is a day I shall remember all of my life. Dr. Graham sermoned that night on Zacchaeus, whose curiosity brought him to Christ; he told of how Jesus had seen Zacchaeus in the tree and had said, 'Zacchaeus make haste and come down' and how he immediately came down. I knew the Lord was giving me my last opportunity to choose either Him or myself. When the invitation was given I went forward and accepted Christ; and to my eternal wonderment, He accepted me. I no longer cared what my friends had to say; this was my last opportunity and I took it.

"One of the most glorious blessings to come to me from this Crusade has been that my friends, whose respect I was afraid of losing by standing for Christ, have all made decisions. We are starting along a new road together. I have discovered I didn't know the meaning of friendship until I accepted the Lord. Our friendship has deepened and matured through Christ and the knowledge and conviction that this is only the beginning is a constant glory to me.

"Another blessing has been my counselor. As I was standing at the foot of the cross that wonderful evening, a girl linked her arm through mine and led me to the counseling room. I thank God for this new friend daily. She, through the precious gift of her time, has helped me keep from stumbling time and again.

"How can I put on a sheet of paper that the Billy Graham Crusade has meant more to me than anything that has come into my life. I have found life. Life is now abundant because of it. When I pray now I feel as if I am talking to someone I know and love, someone who is listening to me and loving me; and when I read my Bible, someone I love and who loves me is speaking to me. Through the Crusade my life has taken on direction. I no longer have to fight my way through darkness. My Lord is here giving me the light and guidance to walk erect with Him, and what can be more glorious than this?

"God has wonderfully used this Crusade and all who are connected with it. As a result of His Spirit working through the Crusade, thousands of church members will be returning to their churches to make them really alive in the Lord. Thousands of unchurched people will be finding for the first time the joy of worship and fellowship with other Christians. Through the Billy Graham Crusade, God has given me a new start and a new heart and will. He has changed my life and the lives of countless others.

To God be the Glory."

Peggy was definitely not the typical New York girl, even though her home had been in the city for a number of years. Peggy did not know who her real parents were. She had been adopted by her foster mother as a baby, before her foster mother was married. "I can never forget the kindness of my mother for taking me in while she was still

single, and giving me a good home all these years," she
said as she thought back on her childhood. "Mother did
everything she could for me. After I had been with her for
a while, she married. I was just eleven at the time, and
I think I resented my new father claiming a part of
mother's affections.

"His coming into the family brought much disappointment to us. He began to drink and his drinking developed
into alcoholism before long. Meanwhile mother was doing
all she could to make up for this sadness. When I finished
high school, she sent me to a finishing school in the south.
I'm sure she did it to give me every opportunity to develop
spiritually and socially. Although it was supposed to be
a religious school, we received much Biblical criticism
while we studied.

"Before long I made some good friends among the
daughters of foreign missionaries. They were very good
girls, but I felt that their religion was too much a religion
of don'ts. Morally they were above reproach, but I do not
recall hearing them mention their relationship to Christ.

"I remember one thing that happened when I was in
the school. Billy Graham was preaching in Charlotte,
North Carolina, and a group of us girls decided to go and
hear him. You see, I was never really opposed to the
Gospel—in fact I was surrounded with the Gospel all my
life. Only I had never been made to see that sometime I
must personally receive Christ. When we got to Charlotte,
we found the meeting-place was filled to capacity, and
we never did hear him. I think I must have had a special
interest in evangelists because my own great grandfather

was a good friend of D. L. Moody. My family always talked about that friendship.

"When my college days were over, I returned to the metropolitan area to rejoin my mother. I had enjoyed the social niceties of the southern school, the good friends, the outdoor activities, horseback riding and many other diversions. But I was glad to get back with mother. I didn't stay with her for long, but got a place of my own with a friend here in the city. Soon I was employed by the director of a famous television show. This was an exciting experience to me. I saw and met many of the celebrities of show business. It was definitely a life that contrasted with the gracious hospitality I had known in the south, but it was much more glamorous.

"Then I began going out with a young man. He had been in show business, and I thought it all very thrilling. We began drinking together, and it wasn't long before that was the usual way we would spend an evening. I can never quite understand how I could have gotten so far away from the training mother gave me or the standards of the college I attended. I never really enjoyed all this drinking. It never did make me really happy to be in on all this kind of thing.

"I remember that last summer a young man kept calling the office to talk with my boss, who was never in. The young man I learned later was Lane Adams. He called so many times that I finally asked him if I might do something for him. He said I could, and invited me to attend the Crusade meeting being held in Madison Square Garden. Although everybody around the office had talked about the meeting, I hadn't been there. So when Lane invited me to go, I decided I would. I had missed Billy in Charlotte, and here was my chance to hear him. Mr. Adams had reserved seat tickets for me and a friend for that night, so I felt we should go.

"Until that night, I had never given any serious thought to the matter of being a Christian. I just supposed I was. I knew I wasn't a Buddhist or a Hindu, so I must be a Christian. Now that I have found Christ, I realize how many people there are in the world who are just as I was. I had just broken up with my boy friend and I was ready for the message in more ways than one. I suppose some people will say that I turned to the Lord because I had been disappointed in love, but that really isn't true.

"As I sat there and listened to Billy Graham, I was most impressed by the challenge of his message. He said that Christ asks for your all, and I knew that I had never given Him my all. I was also deeply impressed by his explanation of the Scripture that says 'All have sinned, and come short of the glory of God.' I never did understand what that meant, but the way he explained it made me see clearly that I was certainly not as good as Jesus, and if not, then I needed a Saviour. Right then a truth dawned upon me that I had never given thought to before. I knew without any doubt that I needed Christ as my Saviour.

"I responded instantly to the invitation. This was what I had longed for all my life, but the matter of making a definite personal decision had never been made so plain to me before. It just seemed natural to go down there to the front of the Garden and openly confess Jesus as my Saviour. It gave to me such a feeling of relief. I was genuinely happy for the first time, for before this I had always been somewhat sad and depressed. I'm not that way any more since Christ has come into my life.

"The next day in the office I told everyone what had happened. One of my friends and I went out for lunch, and we talked about my decision. Now I see it definitely wasn't right, but we sat there drinking beer while I was telling how the Lord had saved me. Drinking had become such a commonplace thing that it never occurred to me that I shouldn't. That was my last drink. God also gave me a good opportunity to witness to my boss. I have talked with him often since then, and he shows a real interest in what has taken place in my life.

"Just about the time all this was happening, the show we were producing lost its sponsor, and when no other sponsor was ready, it was necessary to close the office. That left me out of a job. But I knew the Lord had something in store for me. At one time in my life I would have worried about it, but I had given my life to Christ and had no fears. One Monday night at the Feminar (a group of girls, "babes in Christ," who meet to study the Bible together), Myrl Flood told me of a Christian man who was looking for a secretary. I contacted him and in just a few days I was told to come to work. I am now working for a wonderful Christian man who served as counselor at the Crusade all summer. He is right now planning to lead a Bible-study program for some of the young men in the city who met Christ at the Crusade. I'm very happy in this new position, and thank God for the wonderful way He has been directing me.

"In New York you're usually lonely. But I'm never

lonely any more. I would never have believed that Christ would do that for a person. I have talked with mother many times since the night I was converted. Now I find that we have so much in common. I used to think she was queer about her religious life, but now I realize that it was a faith in Christ that kept her through many troubled years with my alcoholic father. She was always so sweet and uncomplaining. Now I understand why she could bear up under it. Christ was keeping her just as He is keeping me now. My great joy now is to study His Word. This is the realization of all I have longed for through the twenty-four years of my life."

There seems to be no particular age group of the New York working girls who came to the Saviour through the Crusade and found the satisfaction of a living faith. Becky was four years older than Peggy, and her life story was one that had sharp contrasts. As a young girl, the only Christian she ever knew was a Sunday school teacher who took a special interest in her. This was the only Christian influence she could remember. But she acknowledged, "The only reason I thought I was a Christian was that I was not Jewish." Becky did remember, "When I was about twelve or fourteen years of age, I had the feeling that I was very close to God. I loved Sunday school. After that I just drifted away. I began to look upon life from a psychological basis. I talked about what I wanted out of life. I often thought about the meaning of life and wound up hopelessly confused. I have finally discovered the answer since my eyes have been opened, but it was terribly confusing to be thinking so much about these things and not know what the answer was.

"I became bitter toward life and had so much hatred in my heart toward people. Morally I was on the downgrade. Then at twenty I met and married a young fellow who had a church background. I couldn't live with him because of his deceitfulness. I gave my all in marriage only to be rudely awakened by his slippery ways of doing things. At one time his mother became ill, and he left me to go with her. He stayed with her then for quite a while. All this time I was getting reports on his dishonest dealings. Even though I had gone into a moral slump and was drinking a lot, I always had a sense of honesty. That was one virtue I preserved when everything else had gone. Because of this I felt very self-righteous. At the end of three years we parted. We had both been drinking a lot, and in addition we were not always faithful to each other.

"After our separation I went still deeper into sin and openly. I was low, near the end of everything, when the Crusade came to New York. I had heard of Billy Graham, and remembered reading about him when he was in London, but it was just a passing thought then. Now that I learned he was coming to New York, I wanted to hear him. I was very conscious of my sins. Whenever I joined a crowd for a cocktail party I would be very restless.

"The first night I went to the Garden, Billy preached on the Samaritan woman. I knew that message was for me, because I was a sinner like her. So many times after that night, Billy would say that no one came by accident, but by appointment. Well, that night I surely came by divine appointment. Then he also said, 'You may think you are a Christian,' and I was shocked into realizing that I wasn't.

"As he preached, he also mentioned Nicodemus, and told about being born again. I thought, as he preached, how wonderful it would be to start all over. I wanted that chance. I didn't want to be bad, but I couldn't help it. All of these things were going around in my mind, but somehow I didn't really feel the impact of them until he gave the invitation. It was the invitation that got me. I broke into tears as I thought of the terrible life I had been leading. I felt like running to the front of the Garden to take the Saviour that night. The counselor didn't help me too much, but she tried. I was too emotional right then to listen to what she had to say.

"When the next morning came, I thought it would all have passed over, but Christ was a living reality to me. I soon received Bible helps, and began going to the Bible study conducted by Reverend Blinco every night before the Crusade. Then I met some wonderful Christian friends, and beginning that night, everything about my life has changed. Even my job has finally changed. Not that there was anything wrong with it, but I didn't have enough to do. My boss was away so much that I had time on my hands, all of which troubled me. I wanted to earn my salary.

"Then just a couple of months after I had become a Christian, I had an opportunity to take a position with a missionary organization to foreign students. I plan to begin my work with them soon, and all of this has happened since the night I took Christ as my personal Saviour. I am so relieved because I know that my sins are all forgiven, and that the Lord will guide my life from now on."

Such decisions are not the symptoms of adolescence as some have asserted. They are the experience of men and women of every age and from a variety of backgrounds. The surprising similarity that is noticeable between the experience of those who have had a religious background and those who have never known the meaning of the word Christian, indicates that regeneration is a supernatural and not a natural experience that can be accounted for by psychological methods.

Mary, for instance, is only nineteen. She too is a secretary, but has never had the colorful experiences that an older woman would have had. She was still at home with her parents in a beautiful New Jersey town that was nestled close by the Hudson River looking across to the fabulous skyline of Manhattan.

It was with a feeling of sadness that Mary was forced to admit, "I don't know if my parents are Christian or not. They are good people, and I love them dearly. They have given me a wonderful home, and I have lacked nothing. But they almost never go to church, and the Bible is a closed book in our home.

"I have gone to Sunday school, but they don't use the Bible there. It was more a social thing where we girls got together. Our teacher is a wonderful person and we have had some grand times together, but it never was a time of Bible teaching. She counseled us on some of our personal problems and it did help all of us, but as a result, I just *thought* I was a Christian.

"When they were taking in members in the church some time ago, I was in the group that joined. Most of the kids in our class did. I don't know what the rest of them were thinking, but at that time when I stood before the church to be received into the membership, I knew I was lying when I claimed to be a Christian.

"Then a little while after that experience, I was in Ocean Grove. Some girls wanted me to go with them to hear Billy Graham. Our opinion certainly does change, but at that time I thought he was peculiar. I preferred the dignified service in our church, and I also resented the teaching that we aren't saved by our goodness. I was always a good girl, I thought. I admit I did some things that now seem to be out of the question, but then they didn't seem out of order at all. I did smoke; I drank to be sociable but never got drunk. I had learned profanity in the office and swore too much. Worst of all I had a bad temper, but I could always justify that psychologically.

"When a group of girls asked me to go with them to the Crusade last summer, I thought I'd go with them to confirm my opinion of Billy Graham. In spite of my feelings about him at Ocean Grove, I was interested and remembered how I had sat there at that time, gripping my chair as I mentally argued down what he said. I think Billy was just the same as he had been, but somehow the message had a meaning for me it had not had that summer at Ocean Grove. Because the girls encouraged me, I did go forward, though I didn't think so much about it right then. The counselor was a lovely girl, about my own age. She certainly knew her Bible, and that made me realize how little I actually did know about it. She was terrific.

"I didn't feel much different that night, as some people said I would. I didn't have much emotion. But all of that came slowly for me. I did feel relieved, because I had been uncertain for such a long time, and now I at least knew that I had taken a definite step. The best has been since then. Every day, as I study my Bible, and pray, and meet more wonderful Christian friends, I have an increasing joy. I have Christ in my heart, and I know that He'll be with me all the way. Right now my parents think I'm crazy, but they don't object. My mother thought I shouldn't carry my Bible to work every day, but I want to have it so when I have a break I can study it. Also it gives me wonderful chances to tell others in the office why I carry it.

"I had to change churches. I remember that I signed a card the night I went forward, and said what church I would go to. Well, I went, but the preacher made some caustic comments about people going forward in mass meetings like the Crusade, and I knew he wasn't going to help me. I knew that many of the kids I had come to know were going to a little chapel and getting lots of Bible study. They also had outings where they would enjoy wholesome Christian companions. After about two or three of the occasions when my pastor made other slur-

ring remarks about Billy, I left there. My parents were
opposed to my leaving because that is where they go,
when and if they go. They really have gone a little more
since I was converted, and I'm hoping to bring them to
my Saviour before long."

9. Faith Renewed

MANY "G.I.s" came to hear the Gospel. Some came because they were lonely; some because they loved the Gospel, and not a few because they had hungry hearts
beneath a tough exterior. Among those who came were
those who had been taught the things of God from their
earliest childhood. Tim was one of the members of the
armed services. He had come to hear Billy Graham because, as he said, "I tried to hear him in Stuttgart and
Kaiserslautern when he was holding meetings in Germany.
Many of my buddies heard him then, and my heart was
hungry for the things of God."

As a boy, Tim had been given Bible teaching and the
example of Christian friends and church. When he was
twelve years of age he had a keen interest in such things,
and although these had been pushed into the background

of his thinking, they were never completely forgotten. The
Bible was not plainly taught, even in Sunday school, to
the best of his memory, yet there was that influence that
continued to affect his life even during his army days.

"Eight years ago," Tim said, "I did make a decision for
Christ. At that time there was sincere repentance for sin
and true faith in Christ. For a while I had the happiness
one would expect from being converted. In fact at that
time I gave up many of my former bad habits and began
living a clean life. I'm thirty-eight years of age now, so
you see through the years of military service, I didn't mix
too well with younger fellows. Besides I was a specialist,
first class, and was pretty much on my own.

"While in Germany, I met and married a lovely German
girl. She was a member of the Lutheran Church, and regularly attended their services. We have been very happy in
our married life. When we finally came to America, we
began attending a German-speaking church on Staten
Island. She enjoyed that touch of her homeland, but the
language barrier was too great for me. I couldn't get much
from the sermons, because my knowledge of German was
limited to household chatter.

"Without being aware of what was actually happening,
I continued to grow cold in my spiritual life. There was
little more than formality for me, and it was very deaden-
ing. I longed to hear the Bible preached, but for some
reason I didn't go where it was preached, nor did I study
it myself. I can see now that it was for lack of systematic
Bible study that I declined in my Christian life. I was so
backslidden that I could never have given a definite an-

swer if asked whether I was a Christian or not. I firmly believe that I was all the time, because I never went back into the sinful life I had been living before that time eight years ago. I did so much want to hear Billy when he was in Germany, for I knew he would be preaching the Gospel. I was sure that he would preach so that I would come back to the Lord, and I did want that fellowship.

"The trouble was, these times of spiritual desire were separated by long periods of indifference and carelessness. The night I went to hear Billy was the first night of the Crusade. I felt I couldn't miss it, and I went with a desire for complete assurance of salvation.

"I can never forget that night, because it was a definite turning point in my life. As he preached, Billy stressed the importance of being sure. He said, 'If you are not sure of your salvation, you can be sure tonight.' I had been going over these words in my mind again and again. I knew I had made a definite decision eight years ago, but it was as if I had turned away and had crucified Christ all over again. My cold attitude toward Christ had closed my mouth for witnessing, and I doubt if anyone I had met within the last three or four years considered me a Christian.

"As I listened I felt absolutely powerless. I agreed with everything he said, and with my mind I knew it was all true, but I had no power to make a move at all. But as he kept quoting the Scriptures over and over, I found myself responding with ever-increasing faith. It was becoming more and more a vital thing. It seemed to me that the Spirit of God was present, and now I know He was. Once

or twice Billy spoke of the apostles on Pentecost, and how
Jesus promised that they should receive power after the
Holy Spirit came upon them. That verse made a powerful
impact on me, because what I lacked was the power Jesus
promised. I was convinced that I must have that power. I
knew too much about the Christian life to be contented,
and I felt that I would have been better off as a heathen
than a Christian so powerless and cold.

"By the time Billy gave the invitation, I was ready to
go. He didn't ask for Christians to come that night, but
just made a call for the unconverted. But I had to do something before going home. I think my sin of coldness and
indifference must have been worse in God's sight than the
sins of those who had never known the Gospel.

"The young man who counseled me helped me very
much. He had not been converted as long as I had, and
I was so ashamed to have him point out Scriptures that I
couldn't find. He didn't try to show off, but I felt that I
should have been there helping others to Christ, and here
I was in such spiritual need myself. I had nothing to show
for eight years of Christian profession. But as he opened
the Bible and showed me some very fitting Scriptures, I
could feel the presence of the Holy Spirit. Right then he
gave me such enlightenment as I had never had before.
He opened my understanding to verses I had looked at a
few times, and they became alive for me. Following this
sense of enlightenment, I was conscious of such a release
from the soul pressure and such a relief of mind that it
was almost like rising into the air. I experienced a complete freedom from earthly ties. I was more filled with joy

than I had ever been, and I knew it was the joy of the
Holy Spirit. Nothing had changed in my circumstances.
Nothing except a surrender of my whole will to Christ and
a desire for His presence in my life.

"Now at last I have found what I have sought for, even
though I had not known what I was seeking for. It was
a longing for His presence in such fullness as I now have.
I can only say that I am now completely satisfied. I have a
definite assurance of my salvation and know that all my
sins are forgiven. It is a wonderfully clean feeling. In addition to that, I have the promises of God that He will
help me to achieve a victorious Christian life. There is no
feeling other than that of completely belonging to God.
The channeling of the Holy Spirit in our lives becomes
very plainly synchronized, like tuning in on your radio
set. He answers your prayers and gives the certainty the
Bible tells about.

"Because I have not been affiliated with any church, I
couldn't indicate that on my decision card. Having gone
to several churches, I have finally decided where I will
make my church home. I decided on this church because
it is one that invites people to come to the Saviour, and I
can support such a definite effort to win men and witness
for the Lord.

"The Bible is open to me now. At last I can read it with
pleasure and profit. I am learning many things each day,
but more than just learning, I want my life to count in the
future. People who didn't know I was a Christian before
will know it from now on. I'll have to do a lot of explain-
ing when I tell them, but all that has happened to me in

this renewal of my faith has given me more than a knowledge of Christianity; it has given me the power I went so long without."

For many Christians who had been in the Way for a number of years, the Crusade came as a time of refreshing. An Old Testament prophet once cried out to God, "O Lord, revive thy work in the midst of the years." Just as the Crusade was the time of salvation for many who either had never heard the Gospel or had heard and given no heed, so it was a time of rededication and renewal for slumbering believers. Although the decision is quite different, it frequently is as evident to observers of the phenomenon of conversion as the new birth itself.

One such inquirer was Carolyn. She had been a school teacher for several years, and her naturally inquisitive and active mind had brought her to the knowledge of Christ as Saviour before the Crusade began. This is wonderful in itself, for as Carolyn recalled, "My parents were Roman Catholics, but when I was only six years of age, they purchased a business which kept them from attending church, so I grew up with little or no knowledge of religion.

"In college I went to chapel every Sunday. The minister was a wonderful person, and I liked his services because he talked about living a good life and didn't get involved in discussions about Christ. This would have bored me at that period.

"When I started teaching I didn't feel any need to go to church. None of my friends went either. We were too

busy. Life was pleasant and uncomplicated. We felt no
need for God.

"During the Korean War, I went to teach on an air force
base in the Philippines. There I ran into some of the real
issues of life and began to do some serious thinking for
the first time. When you are dancing with a pilot on Friday night and know that by Monday night he'll be flying
combat missions in a jet plane you do a little thinking! The
base chaplain was a good friend of mine, so finally out of
curiosity I went to hear him preach. He was a dramatic
speaker and gave me some ideas about seeking God's guidance for my life. But I didn't know anything about a personal knowledge of Christ. He was just an historical
personality.

"I then went to Japan where I taught for three years.
There I heard a very wonderful army chaplain. I know he
was presenting the truth of Jesus in his preaching, but I
seemed unable to believe. While I was still in Japan, a
very interesting thing happened. Billy Graham came to
hold meetings in Korea. I did not hear him, but some time
time after he had been there, soldiers were coming back
from the front for rest leave in Japan. Some of my friends,
among many others, went to hear him. They came back
with glowing faces and a spiritual victory that was much
more than any military one. I knew by their looks and conduct that they were different. I was deeply impressed,
though even then I did not appropriate it for myself. I
was still an observer and a seeker.

"The time came for me to return home, and I did so
with a feeling of spiritual emptiness. A dear friend was ill,

and I felt so unable to do anything. I was shaken, and once again greatly disturbed. I secured a book that was intended to be helpful to persons just such as I. This book urged Bible reading. I followed the suggestion, and in due time, through the reading of the Bible, I made my decision. I had received Christ as my personal Saviour through what was said about Him in God's Word.

"Before this when I had tried to read the Bible, it had not meant much. Now, suddenly, the pages seemed to come alive. The Holy Spirit must really have been opening my heart because the Bible became to me 'a love letter from God,' to borrow one of the expressions Billy used this summer.

"Although I no longer could be classed as a non-Christian, neither was I an active Christian. For this reason I shall be eternally grateful to God for sending Billy Graham to New York. I needed something and it was not until the Crusade that I came into the full blessing of Christ living in me. I cannot separate them one from the other, for they belong together. The first experience brought joy to me personally and inwardly. Life suddenly took on new meaning, especially in my teaching and personal life, in terms of the power and strength I received to resist former temptation, not with regret but with great joy. My dedication which was made at the Crusade made me realize that this faith could no longer remain an inward thing, but must be shared. The thinking Billy Graham caused me to do, and the sytematic Bible study provided by Crusade follow-up, have given me the ideas and the self-confidence to trust in the Lord with all my heart, and to allow myself to be used according to His will in speaking to others and sharing the wonder of God's love. I cannot overstate what that second decision has done for me, nor what the Crusade did for many students in the school where I teach."

This dedication of Carolyn's made a most significant change in her life. To her friends it has been more obvious than her first acceptance of Christ. The Holy Spirit was given the opportunity He sought to have control of the thought life and the will, making her effective as a Christian. Whereas once she was thought of as a good teacher and friend, now she is recognized as a positive and clear witness for Christ. This is the twentieth-century experience Jesus defined when He said, "But ye shall receive power, after that the Holy Ghost is come upon you: and ye shall be witnesses unto me both in Jerusalem, and in all Judea, and in Samaria, and unto the uttermost part of the earth."

10. In the Evening of Life

THERE IS SOMETHING both sad and wonderful about the aged who came to the Saviour in the Crusade. Among those who had lived through many winters was Mrs. Haus. In her seventy-first year she was born again, and she learned by personal experience that as long as there is life, there is opportunity to turn to God for forgiveness. Though she had lived long, the conversion she experienced has given her a youthfulness of outlook that has been missing for a decade or more with many people of her age.

She had many years to look back upon when she was asked to remember her early years. She could recall the good years at home when she received the best of training and had a happy homelife. One thing was lacking though, and that was religious inspiration. She could remember no Bible study or prayer at home and there was no church in her background that had afforded such teaching. When asked if she had thought of herself as a Christian, she replied as so many others did, "I just assumed I was. I just thought of this country as being mainly Christian, and that unless I repudiated the faith of the founders of the nation, I was a Christian. I can't get over how deceived I was, but then no one ever told me until just the last year or two.

"While I was still very young, I suppose in my teens, my mother became very ill. She was encouraged to go into Christian Science as a religion, and she was in it for many years. I followed her and for twenty-five years was seeking physical healing in Science. My husband never opposed me, but I remember whenever I was ill, I would go for healing to the reader. He would sometimes ask me questions I couldn't answer. Mother had died in a critical illness, and I had had recurrences of my illness for years. I finally lost interest when I received no help that way. From that time on, I didn't go to any church for years.

"We moved to a town in New Jersey some years ago. I

had been a member of a church in Brooklyn for a while, but after coming here I didn't associate with any church. I remember a family by the name of Scott. They lived near us and were very friendly. I remember the one time I went to church I went with them. They invited me to hear a musical, which I always enjoy. When Mrs. Scott talked about being born again, I said, 'I just can't understand,' and dismissed it. As soon as I was alone I wanted desperately to do something about it. I think what troubled me most was that I was getting old. I attended a church one Easter, and the pastor made some remark about people who just came on Easter, and my feelings were hurt so I didn't go back to that church. That experience made me feel panicky. The feeling I had was that of a person walking into a black hole. It was terrible.

"Another thing happened when I went with Mrs. Scott to a tent meeting. I would go with her when it was a musical but I was avoiding preaching. I did notice the happiness of the singers. They were such fine young people. As I left the concert, the minister greeted me, and I told him what wonderful singing it was. He remarked to me that there's more. I didn't know what he meant then, but I certainly do now.

"When Billy Graham came to New York, I decided to go. Mrs. Scott had invited me, and then the boy who takes care of my lawn gave me a reserved seat ticket. I decided to go. In fact I went twice. The second time I went there, I intended to go and dedicate my life to Christ. I can't describe all that went on in my mind. I knew after the first meeting I should have gone forward, and was annoyed that I hadn't done so. When I went forward that second night, I was born again, just like Mr. Graham said I would be. I guess that being born again was so unusual for me because I am so old.

"I was so nervous and excited that night. For one thing, my husband refused to go with me, and that upset me terribly. Having had no children, I lavished my affection on him all these years, and I hoped there would not come a difference between us. He is still not a believer, and it is the one disappointment in the whole experience. I was sure I was doing the right thing, and I have not regretted it for a moment.

"The woman who counseled me was wonderful. She showed me many verses that helped me understand what I must do, and I thank God that I made my decision. I was very upset for several days after that. I had some problems and didn't know how to find the answer. But I know the Lord is helping me now. For the first time in my life I am studying the Bible for two hours every day. It's perfectly wonderful. I know it's true and it really works.

"My husband has been a member of a large lodge for many years. It's all right except when he has troubles. Then he can't follow its teaching. That's the wonderful thing about my life now, the teaching I receive from the Bible helps me every day with my problems. When he gets panicky over things, I ask him why he doesn't use his lodge beliefs. He thinks that my faith is too simple. He can't see that just believing in Jesus can solve so many problems, and I must admit I never could before, either.

"I know I don't have much time left. I am already past

seventy, and when you are that old you know that your time is short. But I study God's Word and find daily comfort. For the first time I'm not the least bit afraid of death because now I know that when it comes, I'm going to be with my Lord."

Mrs. Haus was by no means the only old person who came to receive Christ. Many came with white hair and feeble limbs, but they discovered the meaning of the Scripture which says, ". . . but though our outward man perish, yet the inward man is renewed day by day." It was nearly at the end of this life that Mrs. Haus learned the meaning of eternal life, but for her it was not too late. She had not heard the Gospel clearly explained before. God gave her the ability to repent and to believe when she did hear it. She said this admonition from the Bible might be given to every aging person. "Today . . . while it is called today . . . harden not your hearts."

But whether one has lived through seventy-one years without the Gospel, or whether there has been religious training in youth, as in the case history that follows, there is still the necessity of the new birth. Our Saviour said that "Except a man be born again, he cannot see the Kingdom of God." It is a possibility to be reborn no matter what a person's age may be. Miss Garden had been a public school teacher for thirty-five years, and is now retired. "All my life I have wanted to help people, and one way I did this was to devote my teaching years to crippled children. It required special training, but it gave returns in

personal satisfaction. Nevertheless, I felt all these years
that I was missing something. When I retired from active
teaching, it seemed that something had been lacking in
this kind of work."

As she told of her unusual career as a teacher of crippled and underprivileged children, it was evident that she
was a person who had manifested many of the Christian
qualities and standards without having ever discovered
the inner transformation of which Jesus spoke.

"My parents were strict church members originally,"
she said, "but they did a very strange thing. When they
were married, they left the church. They sent me and my
brothers and sisters to Sunday school, but they made me
bitter when they would not allow me to be confirmed after
the teaching period was over. After being away from
church for some time I began to attend another church,
but again both my parents and the minister frustrated me.

"Some time before the Crusade began, Dr. Dan Potter
spoke to an assembly of teachers. He spoke so feelingly
about spiritual things, urging our cooperation, that I was
eager to help in any way I could, and decided to go to the
Crusade. I couldn't imagine what a religious meeting
would be like in Madison Square Garden, but from the
first time I entered the building, it seemed sacred to me.
I even bought a T.V. set so that I could watch 'Impact'
every night. I never spent a summer in New York in all
of my teaching years. I felt I needed to get away from the
heat and activity and to rest. Nor had I ever been in the
vicinity of the Garden. In fact, I was afraid to go there at
first.

"After the first night, I wanted to go more and more. I listened to the wonderful singing of Bev Shea, and Billy Graham's preaching, but for a long time I didn't think I needed anything. I was considered a very good church member, and presumably had no spiritual need that Billy Graham could supply. I was there to give support.

"One night Billy preached about the blind beggar. My own mother had been blind, and I knew what a terrible thing that was. For the first time I was disturbed, and honestly examined my own heart to see if I might be spiritually blind. From that time on I began to weaken in my own self-righteousness. A few nights later he preached about the Pharisee and the publican. I could see that all the time I had been the Pharisee and not the publican. I had never asked God for mercy. I had always hoped for justice only. I wanted to deserve my eternal reward.

"That night I couldn't resist going to declare my faith when Billy gave the invitation. It was a most wonderful experience. I'm not an emotional person, but always try to consider things intellectually. This time I was absolutely shaken. It was like a Pentecost to me, and the Holy Spirit came into my life. That was on July 19th, and it is my new birthday. I have decided to give the Billy Graham Evangelistic Association a contribution every month on the nineteenth. This will be my way of celebrating my new birthday.

"I enjoyed the rest of the summer more than any summer of my life. I spent my days helping in the Crusade office doing whatever work I could. I started the Navigator's Bible Study and have completed that. Now I am active in my own church in a way I have never been. Several others like myself have made decisions, and our minister has been giving better Bible sermons than he ever gave before the crusade.

"I know that a change has taken place because it works out in so many ways. For one thing, I have had more definite answers to prayers since July 19th than I have had in my whole life. I can see it in my contact with other people. I hadn't had anything to do with my brother and his wife for years, but now they have become so friendly. They came to dinner with me the other night, and we had such a pleasant time. I prayed at the table, giving thanks for the food, and they were deeply impressed.

"The depth—width—intensity of it all is the most amazing experience of my whole life. I feel I have been a Christian for many years, but I know that it has only been since July 19th. The most interesting thing now is that I am planning on taking a friend of mine on the Caribbean tour so she can hear Billy. I'm hoping this way to bring her to Christ. I want everyone to have the same joy and peace I have found in my later years."

11. Teen-Age Turnabout

JUVENILE DELINQUENCY is problem number one at the present time. Never before has the nation been so conscious of the moral and spiritual breakdown of its youth. Nearly every newspaper reports some felony or crime committed by teen-agers. The problem has become one of such magnitude that community groups have been formed to study the matter and government agencies have taken steps to curb the onrush of young people into crime.

Among the many gratifying effects of the Billy Graham Crusades has been the effect upon young people. They are the most serious of all who come to hear the Gospel. During the New York Crusade they attended in large numbers. At the time the press was featuring some teen-agers who had become involved with the law. The entire New York police force was unable to cope with the growing problem, nor did they have an answer to it. But night after night, the problem was being solved for one teen-ager after another as they joined persons of every age to seek the forgiveness God offers through Jesus Christ.

Out of the thousands who came, each one had a story to

tell. Some were stories of the average boy or girl who had not yet tasted the depths of sin. Some were confused with the immensity of life's problems, and others were genuine delinquents. Some were from the finest homes, refuting the theory that a child will be good if given a chance, while others were from broken homes or homes that offered no chance for the growing young boy or girl.

On that night when Joy came to the Saviour, she was not noticed by very many, for she was one more of the teen-agers who responded so enthusiastically. Standing at the front of Madison Square Garden, she was a little more attractive than the average, but none would dare imagine that she had lived more in two years than many live in a lifetime. She was only sixteen the night she made her decision. Until she was fourteen, she had been just another growing girl.

There were religious problems at home which confused her, although other girls have survived religious differences they have seen in their parents. Her mother might have known the truth as a young woman, but lacked adequate stability and assurance to overcome the difficulties caused by living with one who was of a different faith. Neither her father nor mother gave the spiritual support a girl would need in a time of bursting emotions and search for added thrills.

"I went once in a while to a Sunday school," she recalled, "but they talked over my head. I don't remember a single thing they taught me. I don't remember that I even knew the word 'Christian.' They must have used the word, but I don't remember. I don't believe I ever thought about heaven or hell. I did think that somehow everyone would have a last chance.

"Until I was fourteen, I didn't do much differently from other kids my age, but then one of the older boys asked me for a date. Of course any fourteen-year-old would be thrilled to have an older boy take her out. I jumped at the chance. I didn't know then what kind of a person he was, but I learned. He was a 'hood,' and it wasn't long before I was one with him. I remember that on one of the first dates he told me that when a girl gets to be fourteen she should learn to smoke, and so I learned then to smoke. He next told me that I should learn to drink. I did that too.

"I didn't go with that fellow for long. I had many of them; some of them were married men. There were even some cops. That's why when I had skipped school for over a month, the principal sent the cops for me, but they didn't do a thing. They were afraid I'd tell on them. (I'm so glad the Lord saved me. I don't know what would have become of me if I hadn't gone to the Crusade this summer and met Jesus.)

"I joined one of the cycle clubs next. I guess there's nothing wrong with riding a motorcycle. I still like to ride. But this club was one where you just get in as a part of a couple, always a fellow and a girl. You take week-end trips to distant places, and often the whole gang stays together. It's an awful thing. We did all kinds of daredevil things, and I always drove illegally. Boys were a part of my life. Just before the Crusade, our club was planning a week-end trip down in Pennsylvania. I can't tell you all we would have gotten into, but believe me, it wasn't good.

"Another thing I used to do for excitement was to jump trucks. I'd just get acquainted with the truck driver and the next thing he'd ask me to make a run with him. We'd be gone for several days, and no one seemed to notice. At least I didn't think they did. My school work was suffering. I was just about flunking everything. All I could think of was that I'd soon be sixteen and then I could quit.

"Some time last spring I got a new boy friend. He was almost ten years older than I was, and I thought this was great. We were going steady like mad when the next thing I knew we were quarreling and then broke up. I thought how boring the summer would be without a steady. I got a job that would give me some money to do things, and thought that would help. But I was really getting low by this time. I worked in a greenhouse and one day I was nearly desperate. I either had to be running like crazy or I'd get depressed. That day, I took a knife and cut my wrist to end everything. Just as I did, the boss came to tell me there were customers. He quick grabbed a cloth and wrapped it around my wrist and from that day on he never mentioned it. He knew what I had tried to do, though.

"One day when I was wondering what to do with myself, a girl named Barbara came and asked me to go to hear Billy Graham. I didn't know who he was, but this girl was one of the nicest girls in our class. She had always been nice to me and I couldn't refuse. She was a clean kind, and I was surprised that she would ask me to go with her. I'm so glad I did, because that night was the turning point. I hate to think what might have become of me if I hadn't accepted her invitation. I went to the Garden with a gang of kids who seemed to be such a clean bunch. I knew how bad I'd been, but I didn't think they knew.

"I can never forget that night. I sat with the kids and listened to Mr. Graham preach. He spoke so plainly to all of us teen-agers. I could understand him. I never could understand that preacher I went to hear back home. He preached over our heads all the time. Mr. Graham told us just how to be saved. He made the Bible seem so simple. I wonder why I never understood it before.

"For the last ten minutes of his sermon, I was glued to my seat. I had never heard about being born again. I thought that if there is such a thing, I needed it, because I had lived such a bad life for two years. I had asked mother a couple of times about religion. She didn't seem to know very much. I felt such a need at times, and then it would go away. But this night it was different. I held on to my seat real hard. I didn't want to go down there, but then I was afraid to refuse. Billy had preached on a text that said something like 'keep thyself pure.' This I had not done, and I knew I'd be lost forever.

"Finally, I just couldn't sit still. I got up out of my seat and started. Before I had ever arrived down front, I knew God was going to forgive all my sins, and make a new person out of me. He did it that night. Before the night was over, a counselor, a swell girl, had showed me in the Bible how God would cleanse me and make me totally new. It was right there in the Bible, and I just believed what it said.

"That night on the bus going back to our town in New Jersey, we sang. We didn't sing the bad songs the cycle gang would sing. We sang about salvation and about Christ. We sang the song that Bev Shea had been singing, "How Great Thou Art." God was great to me that night, and He has been ever since. Other kids with us were saved that night, and we all told how it happened. It was a wonderful experience.

"Some people think it doesn't last, or that it isn't real. Well, that's because they never met Christ as I did. I remember that our teacher assigned a paper for us in English. We were to write on the topic 'Choosing a Friend.' Every other paper I had ever done in that class had been on fixing a motorcycle or how to drink beer. This time I wrote on my choice of a new friend and that friend was Jesus. At first some of the kids in the class snickered a little, but as I read on, they got quiet and listened. My teacher gave me an "A" that time. She was a Christian, but I never knew it before. She told me how ashamed she was to have been my teacher and never to have told us she was a Christian, when I told the class the first chance I had. She certainly has changed a lot since then, too. She even comes to our Hi-B.A. classes (High School Born Againers).

"I want all the kids in school now to know that I'm a Christian. Like the other Hi-B.A. kids, I carry my Bible on top of my other books to every class. When I get my work done, I study the Bible in study hall. Some people think that if I do that I won't get my work done, but I'm getting "A's" in every class now. I used to fail just about all of them. That is just one of the many ways the Lord helps when you really go all out for Him.

"I guess the best thing that has happened is that my father has been brought to the Lord this summer. My mother has been wonderfully renewed in her faith, and now I'm praying that my brother will be saved. He is the only one left in our family who isn't saved now."

As Joy went on talking, she appeared to be a clean, fresh youngster who had never known the depths of sin. Unless she had related the seamy side of her life, one would never have accused her of immorality and wickedness. So complete was the work of God's grace in her that she had the appearance of purity. In God's record she was, for He had blotted out her sins forever. As the interview concluded, the phone rang in the office. It was a call from her brother. She had been praying for him. He called to ask if it was too late to join the group of kids on an outing they were having that night. In a short time they were off, all fifty of them, and Joy in the crowd. She had discovered that she not only had the joy of salvation within, but she had found a wonderful bunch of Christian young people for fellowship, and she was leading her brother into this atmosphere.

A story such as that of Joy's would seem fantastic unless similar stories had been told. Her conversion would appear to be the emotional surge of a moment unless there were many others whose conversion has manifested the permanence that is so clearly defined in the Scriptures.

Paul once wrote, "For I am persuaded, that neither death, nor life, nor angels, nor principalities, nor powers, nor things present, nor things to come, Nor height, nor depth, nor any other creature, shall be able to separate us from the love of God, which is in Christ Jesus our Lord."

Judy was only thirteen when Billy Graham invaded London in 1954 with the Gospel. Like most youngsters she had little past history to tell. Unlike Joy, she had not gone out into the hoodlum life for a whirl, but had lived a comparatively uneventful life. Though her mother had died when Judy was only eight years old, she had lived very comfortably at home with her father and a brother.

"My brother at one time urged me to go to church with him," she said, "but I didn't care to go. Not long after that he dropped out; we were not church-going people. I don't know why I should have thought that I was a Christian at all, but I did. I know now that I was not, but it was something I never gave too much thought to. I was living a good life. I didn't even have the sense of any need, but just thought I was all right. I can't even remember anything that disturbed my rather even way of life that would cause me to think of spiritual things.

"Then one day a friend asked me if I would like to hear an American evangelist. I wasn't sure what it would be like, but I was willing to go. It was the day of the final rally, and we planned to go to White City Stadium. When we got there, we were too late to get in, but we were told that there was going to be another meeting in just two hours at Wembley. Not until then did I get excited about it, but I remember how we hurried. I had the feeling of being left out of something as we hurried from White City to Wembley.

"I was impressed by the singing of such a large crowd. They sang with deep meaning, and I was greatly moved as I listened. I didn't know the songs myself, for I had not been with Christians very much. Although I can't remember the sermon, I do know that I was drawn to go forward when so many others were going. I didn't know a thing about the Bible, and can only remember John 3:16 being mentioned, though Billy gave many other verses. The counselor gave me I John 5:11,12, and explained that a person can be sure of eternal life. I wanted to be sure more than anything else in the world.

"That was nearly four years ago, and I have continued to grow in the Lord ever since. The study of the Bible has been a source of strength to me all along. I have had the usual problems that any young person may have, but the Lord has been with me all the way."

Judy then told of her church where a man of God preaches the Word, and where every Lord's day many who come had, like Judy, met Christ in the Harringay meeting. She was in New York, and gave her time in the Crusade office, mailing letters, answering the telephone, and doing many jobs that contributed to making the Crusade in New York possible. Her plans for the future included always the will of God for her life. Now just a little more than sixteen years of age, she is a living witness to the power of the Gospel of Christ to save and to keep those who come to him, whether young or old.

Teen-agers demand that life be exciting. More than at any other time of life there is the danger that life might become boring. The boundless energy and enthusiasm of boys and girls at that period of life is fraught with both peril and opportunity. Solomon had correctly appraised youth when he admonished them to remember the Creator at that stage in life. In reality, nothing but a vital and challenging faith is sufficient to control and satisfy at that time. Jesus Christ has met the need of every young person who has turned in faith to the cross. There they find cleansing and forgiveness in the blood of Christ.

Pete was one of those refreshing teen-age boys who discovered the way of gladness and light in the Billy Graham Crusade. It was learned that he was in the top ten per cent of his class, an honor student in high school, and active in sports. He was manager of both the football and basketball teams in his school. He also was a lover of baseball, like so many typical American youths. This love for baseball made it seem quite natural for him to attend the Rally at Yankee Stadium, though he had avoided other meetings.

When he was asked about his background, he said of his parents, "I don't know if they are Christians or not. I have really wonderful parents, but they don't go to church regularly. They just don't seem to be very interested. I can't say if it's a lack in them or in the church. They have given me a good home, and though they haven't been really strict, still I have to give an account of my activities.

"It was about two years ago when I first went to a Sunday school. At that time some buddies of mine asked me to go with them. I was interested mainly because I found that there were a lot of my friends in the same class. But there wasn't much Bible teaching, as I remember. The teacher encouraged us to live wholesome, clean lives. Once in a while we'd get a Bible story as an example of clean living, like the one about Daniel when he was in the king's service. I don't remember any others particularly. I guess that one impressed me most.

"To tell the truth, I don't believe I ever gave any thought to the matter of being a Christian. I just didn't stop to think that I might not be. With good parents who were church members, and having no bad habits, I guess I took it all for granted. Once in a while I would think about God, but it was more like being in a class when we got into some question of philosophy. Once in a while I would pray, but it really didn't mean much. I thought that if there were a God, He wouldn't have time to be bothered with my problems anyhow. Boy, I really have changed my mind about that. I sure know He's interested in me now!

"The thing that finally got me to go to the Billy Graham meeting was the meeting at Yankee Stadium. Some of the fellows at school had been going to the Garden, but I didn't like the idea. I thought Billy Graham was some kind of a fanatic. I had been to the Stadium many times, and I guess I just thought it would be O.K. to hear him there. I didn't like the idea of getting closed in a building with him and the others whom I thought were fanatics. I didn't feel that way about these fellows who asked me to go, but I somehow thought they were going just to watch.

Besides, I have always been a Yankee fan, so it made it easy. Even on the bus I tried to figure a way to get out of it, but when we got there and I saw such a crowd, I went along with the gang.

"When the meeting got started, I thought I was going to see a demonstration of mass hypnotism. I had steeled myself against any such thing. For one thing, I hated to admit to my classmates that I had given in to it. I had been such a skeptic before. But there was something about the way Billy preached that just hit home. For one thing, he said there was only one road, and he proved it from the Bible. Even though I hadn't read the Bible much, it made a real impression on me. Then I thought about the Vice President being there, and he was a "VIP" so far as I was concerned. I thought there must be something to it after all. Nixon wouldn't go there for some fanatical religious meeting. The real thing was, I was surprised somehow that a man that important would be religious.

"The next thing Billy said was that now was the time. He said, 'This is your hour with God,' or something like that, and then explained that you couldn't just say you'd come when you were ready or felt like it. You had to come when the Spirit was drawing you. I'm not sure I knew what all that meant, but I felt more and more that if there were anything to it, I had better do something about it right away. Right while I was thinking about it he suddenly said, 'It may be your last chance.' I thought that I was young and had lots of time, but then I thought that guys my age had died or been killed or something had happened to them. Then just about when I had decided not to make a decision right at that time, I stood up. Billy had said for all to stand who wished to receive Christ as Saviour. I just stood.

"Some people don't think that just standing means anything. Well it sure does, because when I stood, I was ready to be saved. It happened in such a short time, and I didn't know much about it, but I knew that I wasn't a skeptic any longer. I was a believer in Christ. My buddies got their Bibles out and showed me verses that explained it to me. I always thought they were funny to carry Bibles every place, but I was really glad they had them right then. That was what clinched it for me.

"I was different from some. I didn't cry or feel any emotion that way, but I was excited. It was really a great experience. It seemed that I didn't have any troubles or problems left. Nothing bothered me at all. All the way home we sang Gospel songs and kids told what they had done that day. There were others saved in our bus load too, and that helped me a lot right to begin with.

"Since that day everything has been so much better. Life has meaning now. I was so mixed up before, because I always tried to give an explanation for everything in terms of science. Now I see you can't do it without God. I have been taking my Bible with me to school, and witnessing to the kids, especially to the football team and basketball team that I manage. It's really great.

"My parents think I'm taking it too far. Either I didn't believe at all and didn't go to church at all or else I spent all my time in church and reading the Bible. I know they think I'm radical, but I don't think so. It's just that I get the most fun out of witnessing and studying the Bible. I am glad that you're going to write up this story so some other guys can know that it really works.

"I don't know what I'm going to do when I get out of school, but I think I'd like to be an athletic coach in some high school. I know how important the coach is to fellows, and that would be a place where I could really make my life count for Christ. I'm going to pray a lot about that."

There is no fitting conclusion to the story of Pete, for he is just at the beginning of a challenging life with Christ. He has not chosen an easy thing. He has chosen the narrow road, but it is the road that leads to life everlasting. Against the indifference of lukewarm Christians and the opposition of skeptics he has decided to walk with God and accept the challenge of going against the current. As he told his story of stepping out of skepticism into faith, there were more than fifty other vibrant, noisy fellows and girls standing outside the little office. They were waiting to come in, one at a time, to tell the story of how they too had found Jesus Christ and the meaning to life.

There are those who say that conversion in youth is not real conversion while others say it is merely a phenomenon of adolescence. Eighteen thousand teen-agers recorded their decision for Christ in four months at the Billy Graham Crusade. Critical observers will wonder what will remain of their decision in the years ahead. One answer is given in the testimony of Carol, who made her decision at the Syracuse Crusade in 1953. Carol was thirteen at that time.

In a letter she said, "My parents, in the normal response of those under conviction, disliked the 'show' and refused to go again. For that reason I didn't go forward, but asked some friends if I could go with them to the meetings. I did go, and later I accepted the Lord without going forward in the meeting. I'm sure it was just as real and sincere. I hope you'll notice the way I was converted because I think many do not realize how many come to the Lord through the ministry of Billy Graham without going forward."

Carol was one of many teen-agers who had no religious background. Her parents had no church contacts, nor did her friends. She wrote, "I did once attend a church camp for a day. Though there was no Bible teaching or even religious meeting, it started me thinking. When I came to the Billy Graham meeting and heard the Bible preached, I knew that I must accept the Saviour. That was four years ago, and since then we have moved away from Syracuse. Now in Phoenix, Arizona, I am active in Youth for Christ work and Bible clubs. Next summer I plan to work as a camp counselor, and then in the fall I am beginning my college studies to prepare for Christian service wherever the Lord may lead.

"I'll never stop thanking the Lord for sending Billy Graham to Syracuse way back in 1953. I'm only one of hundreds helped by that Crusade, but I wanted you to know my story and to know how grateful I am."

To be sure, a few have fallen by the wayside, but it is

not unreasonable to expect that many of the eighteen thousand teen-agers who recorded their decisions will in the future indicate their gratitude to God for the Gospel they heard that brought them to the light. On two occasions, gatherings of young people were visited, and their testimonies recorded. After five months they manifest a joy and a vitality in Christian living that indicates a genuine conversion.

In a youth meeting in White Plains, among those who told of their decision was Elaine. Although she was only fifteen, she had traveled from Uruguay, where she was born, to Paraguay, then to Germany and finally to America. Her father's position in the government had caused the family to reside in these various countries. Her grandmother had taken her to church on occasions. Her mother went to church intermittently, but her father never attended. In Germany she had opportunity to attend the American Sunday school, and did receive a superficial knowledge of the Bible.

"When one of my girl friends came to ask me to go to hear Billy Graham, and told me she had tickets for both of us, I decided to go along with her. Some other girls were going, all of them Christians. They didn't say much to me about becoming a Christian, but now I know they had a definite purpose in asking me.

"I can never forget the shock I received when Billy began to preach. I expected to see something quite different. He was so serious, even insisting on absolute quiet and no moving around during the service. His prayer was so definite for the lost people, and I began to wonder if perhaps I might be one of those lost ones. His sermon broke all my idols. I don't remember his text, but I remember he did make sin such a real part of experience that I realized that I was as great a sinner as anyone.

"I received Christ the second night I attended. I had always known that Jesus came to save the world, but it was never the personal relationship I now have with Him. It was a wonderful experience, the most wonderful in my life. Some people wept, but for me it was nothing to cry about. After that night I attended regularly and only missed two meetings.

"Since that decision, I have been living the Christian life. I have met some wonderful Christian friends in Hi-B.A. and attend their meetings every week. We meet every day in school. Now I take my Bible to school so other kids will know where I stand. At first my parents thought it was just a fad, but after six months they know there is something to it. I have some days of discouragement, but when I read my Bible I am happy all over again. I just wish every young person could know how grand it is to know Christ as I have come to know Him."

Several other teen-agers that night told of their conversion. All of them had been in touch with either church or Sunday school, but none could remember any Bible study or Scripture memorization. In nearly every instance, they made their decisions after the first night, sometimes listening for two or three nights. All of them reported a wonderful new joy they had found through the knowledge of salvation. Their fears were gone, and the uncertainty of growing boys and girls was exchanged for a certainty that gave them all a deep peace.

Similarly in a New Jersey suburban town, a group had gathered at the home of a Christian dentist. Fifty young people were there, all of whom had experienced conversion during the Crusade. They had lost none of their teenage buoyancy and drive, but to that they had added a spiritual insight that made it a singularly inspiring sight. All would have told their stories, but there was opportunity for only a few. Among them was Jack, an honor student in the local high school.

He said, "As a growing boy, religion meant nothing to me. I did go to Sunday school just to be with a group of fellows I liked, but we never talked religion. I can remember that in the Bible there were four Gospels, and from them we heard some historical stories. I never knew that Christ died for me, and no one ever told me about it. I never knew I needed God."

Jack had made his way on the high school gridiron team. He was varsity line backer, and regarded as one of the best players in that section. He also made his mark in wrestling and track events.

He said, "I don't believe I knew anything about Billy Graham before. One of the fellows in school invited me to come. I respected this boy, and then when he said it was free, I decided to go. I knew it must be a great event if they were holding it at Madison Square Garden."

"Until that night I had always assumed I was a Christian. The word really had no meaning as it does now. Now I know I wasn't a Christian. The first thing that shocked me was when Cliff Barrows read the words to a hymn. I had heard the hymn but had never paid any attention to the words. They were wonderful. I also couldn't help but notice that a lot of people were carrying Bibles. Some like myself must not have used them much before. I also saw that people were smiling and very happy.

"I was all mixed up in my own mind, but I wanted to get things settled. I felt like I was turning around inside. The devil was on one side and God on the other. That night I was converted. It took me a week to realize all that had happened. After that I went every night. I suppose the reason I had been so mixed up was that I was practically ignorant of the whole truth about God. The few times I had been to church it was either to be with my friends or to date one of the girls. I was as much without Christian knowledge as a pagan.

"Now that I have been saved, I believe all the Bible. I went to one church where a preacher said that the Bible contains portions of the Word of God. I didn't believe that, so I went to another one where the Bible is studied as the Word of God. God has given me power to witness. I want to tell everyone in school about the way of salvation. I notice all the words in the hymns too, since that night when Cliff read them. I put my Bible on top of my school books and mother thinks that is really too much, but I'm not ashamed of my Lord or His Word.

"Our next project is a high school assembly. Some of us

Christian kids have been given a time for a high school assembly. I'm planning on leading the singing and I'm going to read the words of the hymns before we start to sing them. I'll bet some of the kids have never noticed the words to some of the songs we sing."

Jack finished telling how the Lord had directed in his life, and it was learned from those who knew him that he had come to be known in school for his testimony. His exceptional record demanded the respect of teachers and students alike. No doubt Jack has called attention to the Gospel in a sphere of life where it is seldom mentioned.

Much like him was another fellow called Rudy. He affirmed that his sister was saved, but that the rest of the family were nominal Christians. From his occasional visits to Sunday school he had learned very little.

"A girl friend invited me to go to the meeting," he said, "and she had been saved earlier in the summer. She had shown me the great change that takes place when you believe the Gospel. Until that time I had never thought much about being a Christian. Once in a while I would wonder about God, but not too much. I would once in a while pray, but they were very selfish prayers. I never did read the Bible, so you see I didn't have much to begin with.

"The night we went to hear Billy, I was convicted. I determined not to go forward, and when others were going, I sat there. Finally I couldn't hold out any longer, and I joined those who were going. I wasn't sure what it meant, but I definitely wanted to find out how they could help me. I soon found out, for another fellow about my age sat with me down in the Counseling Room, while a minister spoke to us about how to be saved, and then the fellow let me ask any questions I wanted to, and every one he answered by finding a verse in the Bible. The surprising thing to me was the way those verses seemed to fit exactly. One I remember was from Ephesians that said, 'For by grace are ye saved through faith; and that not of yourselves: it is the gift of God: Not of works, lest any man should boast.' I was definitely helped by that verse, and have since read it over and over.

"That night I was happier than I had ever been. Right away I wondered if it would last, because it seemed too good. It has lasted, I'll tell the world. I'd never want to go back to the old way of life. I was really a poor example for a young guy while growing up, and the Lord has changed all that."

Similar stories might be told by more than eighteen thousand young people of the metropolitan area. Many of those who took their stand for Christ were students in colleges in various parts of the city. But there were also many who were students in colleges in other places around the United States, who had received Christ either while watching television during the Crusade, or who happened to be visiting New York, or were home on summer vacation. These could not be personally interviewed, but in letters they told of the wonderful things God had done for them.

Andy, a student at Colgate University wrote saying, "This experience changed my life. Although I was active in church life, my knowledge of the Bible was superficial. I considered myself a Christian, but that was because I never knew what a Christian was. I went to hear Billy Graham because I thought that I should, but after the third night I answered the invitation. Once I had made the decision, I wanted to go out and witness all over New York. Many fellows here at the university need the Lord, and I pray that I will be able to lead them to Christ."

Another student, Thorny, wrote saying, "Christian influence as I now know it, I never had. I always compared myself with those around me, and that made me feel that I must be good enough. My mouth and mind were filthy, but since coming to the Lord, He has helped me in this problem. The whole experience made me very thoughtful, and I now have a determination to live for Christ."

Of these students who wrote telling of their experiences during the summer, one particularly well-written statement was made by a young student at Yale University. Don had no religious background to speak of. At the most he had been in Sunday school about six times as a young boy. At thirteen he joined the church for "propriety," but found the sermons void of spiritual content though they were intellectually stimulating. The only basis upon which he judged himself a Christian was that he was not a communist.

One evening, Don had a date whom he wished to impress with one of the big activities in New York. He said, "My life before the Crusade was one of flashy play-acting to cover up the inner depression and sense of futility. The inadequacy of human striving and my own sense of little accomplishment brought me to realize my own unworthiness in the world. As we sat there and listened to Billy, it seemed that the living voice of Christ was speaking to me. The simultaneous disgust and concern with knowledge of a philosophical nature led me to recognize the necessity of a changed life. My multitude of unsolved problems made me realize that I was unable to face things in my own strength.

"As I weighed all the possibilities, and thought of the responsibility I had, I realized that Christ had the right to be my true master. Billy taught so plainly that His love had been expressed in His life and death, and that this act called for my complete surrender. As he spoke, I became convinced, and when he gave the invitation I answered by going forward. I knew that going forward didn't save me, but, as Billy explained it, it was my public witness to Christ. As I sat with a young man who counseled me, I was happy because I was now assured of absolute justification and had a purpose for living. I was ready to sacrifice any material gain to maintain this wonderful relationship to Christ.

"Six months later, as I look back on this event in my life, it still means to me that I decided to follow the Lord at any cost. Little did I know how impossible this would be without His strength. The Holy Spirit has given me this strength. I have learned to trust in Him, not only for guidance, but for the power to resist temptation."

As testimonies of various types of people are considered, it becomes increasingly evident that the work of grace in the hearts of men is not limited to any particular temperament or social class or age group. The redemption from sin through Christ is for all. The Gospel knows no class or race, but at the cross, all men are equal.

12. Conversion Unclassified

MEN OF THE ARMED services have felt the impact of the Billy Graham Crusades. Many of them have turned from darkness to light and have found a peace with God. When the Billy Graham Crusade was on in Shreveport, Louisiana, one of them was included with the many who received the Saviour. His is one more story of the triumph of the Gospel, and displays its effectiveness to men and women everywhere. "Ye are our epistle written in our hearts, known and read of all men," was the commendation that Paul so highly regarded, and it might also be said of the ministry of God's servant Billy Graham.

Today Bob is a minister of the Gospel. Six years ago he was going the way of destruction. His home life as a boy provided no spiritual instruction, and although there were some morals taught in his family, the father set a poor example by drinking. Bob's life until the time of his conversion was without the element of special interest. He grew up with no more nor less than the average boy or girl.

Then came the time when he must serve in the armed services. Before long he was a military policeman. This gave him more than his share of pride and haughtiness. But in spite of the toughness of his armed services job, he was fearful within. On one occasion, when he was stationed in Denver, he attended church, heard the Gospel and refused. This sent him into deeper sin than he had known before. This was his only contact with the Gospel, and it was to be several months before he would again hear it clearly.

Bob continued his work as an M.P. when he was sent to a camp near Shreveport. His usual Saturday night diversion was to visit the tavern and drink. As he sat there that night, a Salvation Army lassie entered and distributed the periodical, *War Cry.* Bob was greatly disturbed by her coming in. He felt she should not enter such a place, but then he almost at once asked himself the question, "Why am I here?" Bob jumped up from the table where he was sitting and went to explain to the young woman. To her he said, "I'm sorry I'm in this place." This was his true feeling. Like most men living in sin, he did not approve of his own conduct.

Bob recalled, "One week end I promised to attend Sunday school, but I was out the night before drinking, and didn't get in until after 3:00. I was both drunk and broke. I couldn't get up for Sunday school. That afternoon, a friend came into the barracks and called, "Who wants to

hear Billy Graham?" My conscience was bothering me because I hadn't gone to Sunday school when I was invited,
so I thought this would take the place of it. I didn't know
what Billy Graham was like. I had an idea that he was
some old, whiskered man like a grandfather. So I went.
As we drove along, I remember passing a little tent, and
thought my friend had accidentally driven by the meeting
place. Soon we came upon the huge place where the crowd
was gathering, and we went in. I'll never forget how I
felt. I wondered what to expect that could cause such a
crowd to come to hear him.

"The meeting got under way, and it seemed very short.
In thirty minutes it was over, or at least I thought so. Then
my friend explained to me that this had only been the
Hour of Decision broadcast. I was glad that there was
going to be more. In spite of my wicked life, I had a desire
to know God and to have peace in my own soul.

"When the regular service began, Billy Graham changed
his style. He had been preaching machine-gun style about
world affairs and their meaning. Now he began to search
my soul. His preaching was so direct that I couldn't miss
its meaning. I remember that he said, 'There's a heaven
and there's a hell. You'll go to hell unless you're born
again.' I think his text was 'Prepare to meet thy God.' I
knew well the rottenness of my own soul. He said, 'God
didn't spare Sodom, He didn't spare the world in Noah's
day, He didn't spare His Son, and He won't spare you.'

"I held on to my seat while Billy gave the invitation. I
can't explain why, but I did. I said to myself I wouldn't go,
even though it was what I knew I should do. I was having

a terrific battle that only the Lord and I knew anything about. Billy had closed the invitation, and I still sat there. Suddenly I wasn't able to resist any longer. I felt as if the earth would swallow me up. Something pulled me out of my seat, and then I actually ran to where the people were standing.

"I found the Saviour that night, but I didn't have the easy time some do. I felt that there was still something lacking in my life. I didn't let go of some of my old habits even though I felt that they didn't belong to the Christian life. I thought I could hold on to them for a while until an old Negro asked me why I continued in the wicked ways if I had been saved. This condemned me. I knew that something had taken place in me, or I would have become violently angry with the old Negro. As it was I thanked him for the help he gave me.

"Then I went to find a church home. I went to one church, and as I was leaving the morning service, the minister invited me to some affair that afternoon. He said there would be some cookies and some girls there. I told him that I had come for more salvation. I was afraid to go back to the old life, so I sought for more than social contacts.

"For more than a year I sought for this fullness. I visited some of the churches that preached such a doctrine, but found that they did not help me. They told me that I must seek sinlessness, for if I sinned I'd be lost. This troubled me night and day. I was saved and lost so many times, I thought, until finally I came to see that Christ had made atonement for all my sins.

"After more than a year of such struggling, I finally came to rest in the complete work of Christ. I knew that my salvation depended upon His merit, and not on mine. When I had finally realized that fact, God gave me a wonderful peace. But almost at once I felt the burden to preach the Gospel. A series of events finally brought me to Bible school and college. I found a wonderful girl who has been a constant inspiration to me in the work, and today, after these years have passed, I feel I must give all the glory to God who brought me to know His own Son in the act of faith in the Shreveport Crusade. Some have asked me whether the conversions made at the Crusades last. I am a living flesh-and-blood example of one of the many who did last. God has given me a ministry to others, and I am happy to be preaching the Gospel. God has opened the door, and I am one of the many who attributes his salvation to the ministry of Billy Graham. It is not that we are converts of Billy Graham. We have been converted to Christ, and those who come to Christ are never ashamed nor do they have the desire to go back to the old life."

It was clear that God had brought this young man along a winding pathway of spiritual confusion in order that he might become an understanding minister of Jesus Christ. By experience he has learned the ups and downs of the new convert. He knows that the way is not an easy way, but he also has learned that the power of the Gospel is supreme. He has learned how to direct the struggling believer into the rest and peace provided through the blood of Christ. Today, he preaches the same everlasting Gospel that his spiritual father preaches. His ministry is to a local church, but he preaches the same Saviour from sin, and the same glorious hope that Billy expounds.

Jesus is described in the Bible as "a cornerstone in God's plan." Antonio could understand such language well, for he had learned the bricklaying trade and had been with builders most of his life. As a young man, he knew only those people who believed that being a Christian meant going to church every Sunday. Now he has learned that "church-going" is a good thing, but believing and trusting in Christ is the way of salvation.

"I never learned much Bible," he said, "but just heard that there is a God that people should worship. I never learned much about Him. I did not know that God loves us like His children and leads us. I thought that there just was a God somewhere in heaven that would some day judge us. I even thought He was a very mean person that we could never talk to. I was afraid of God, and went to church because I expected a judgment some day. But as much as I went to church, I could never remember from one week to the next, anything I had heard.

"The Billy Graham meeting was not promoted in my church. Some of the people would mention it, but generally they were like myself, just curious. I think all the time I had a hunch that Billy Graham was a true man of God. I had listened a couple of times to his radio program. It sounded as though he were telling the truth but there were so many other things going on that I never listened to a whole sermon.

"I was a very wicked man. Working continuously with swearing and drinking men gets you that way yourself. All the guys at work told rotten stories. Once in a while if a fellow tried to be good we made fun of him and called him a sissy. But I never got in trouble with the law or anything. I was just a terrible fellow who didn't know God, worked and drank hard, and didn't care about what I did. My religion didn't say I had to do good. At least I never thought it did. I guess I was a pretty poor church-goer.

"One day a friend asked me to go to hear Billy Graham. I hadn't thought about going before that. I went with the friend and I'm glad I did. There was no truth in all the things I had heard against Billy Graham. I believe he is a real messenger of God, and I prayed that I could come as close to God as he is. That was how I felt the night we sat there and listened the first time. It's hard to describe my life before that night, it was so bad; all I know is what has happened to me since. Praise God forever!

"Billy Graham preached from a Bible verse which I had heard before. It said, 'Except ye . . . become as little children, ye shall not enter into the kingdom of heaven.' Billy said it was not enough to change our religion, but that we have to change our hearts. I guess what got me most was that he used the Bible so much. I had never heard a preacher do it that way. I believed the Bible, but never had read more than a couple of verses in it. I don't know why I did believe it. I had even thought I was a Christian, but I had never known what a true Christian was or how he should live.

"When Billy preached that night, I felt as though God

were speaking to me. That was because of his using the
Bible as he did. For the first time in my life I examined my
conscience. I saw myself for what I really was. I had
never in my life seen a preacher have people come forward
like that, and I wasn't sure about going. I suddenly just
got up without thinking much about what I was doing
and went. I was a little scared because I didn't know what
to expect. I did know I wanted to have my life changed
and be a child of God. I knew that church-going had
never changed me one bit.

"Well, I finally was down in the room where all the
people went to talk about receiving Christ. A fellow
talked with me, but I don't think he understood my problem too well. He did show me some good verses that
helped me, and prayed that the Lord would make me
understand. He gave me some little cards with verses on
them. What he said seemed to help me, because when I
left Madison Square Garden that night, my whole life
seemed different. I was a desperate person when I went
in there, but I got a new outlook on life. I became a patient
person, trusting the Lord and I have faith that He will
deliver me from all temptations.

"This was the greatest thing that ever happened to me.
It made me find my Lord. I was reborn. Glory to God! I
pray that what happened to me can happen to others."

Although this last statement of Antonio's had been said
by hundreds of others, it was the natural thing for him to
say. He had found the peace that passeth understanding.
He was one of the many working men who sought and
found Christ. There is no single class of people for whom

the Gospel is specially adapted. Whether it is the laboring man, the office worker, or the housewife, there is a message of hope for all in the Gospel. ". . . it is the power of God unto salvation to every one that believeth." Every social barrier is broken down and class distinction removed when men and women seek the Lord in meetings such as the Billy Graham Crusades. Antonio discovered this to be true, and although there are many problems for him still to face, he has found the One who has the solution to life's problems.

Being a housewife in some sections of New York can be a boring and frustrating experience. Hildegard is only twenty-eight, and it looks as if her future would be to go along from day to day, looking out of an apartment window and seeing nothing but another apartment house exactly the same as the one in which she lived. She has a husband who is not a believer, but he enjoys speculating in various religions and philosophies. He attended the Billy Graham Crusade with her, but his heart was not opened to the Word of the Lord, and he is unchanged to all outward appearances. God alone knows the conviction and concern that may well have had its beginning when he heard the Word of God preached and with his own eyes watched hundreds do what he refused to do.

Hildegard also has a baby. He is the pride of her life, and she finds great joy in him. Judged by almost any standard, she would be a model housewife and mother. But like all others who come to the Saviour, she has a memory. Now that everything about her had changed, she would still remember all that went beforehand in her life until the night when the big change took place.

First of all, she remembered that her mother was a Christian. In Germany, where she was born, the state church claimed many in its membership who knew nothing of God's grace and who were strangers to God. She still believed that her mother was different, and that she was more than just a nominal member of the church. She was a woman who prayed earnestly for her children, and could be seen often pouring over Luther's translation of the Bible as an occasional tear would fall and stain its pages. Her father was not like that, but was cold and formal, even to his children.

"The Bible was a book just for old people," thought Hildegard, even though she had been confirmed and baptized. "I can remember a few verses I learned at that time, but for years I haven't thought of them at all." This is so typical of many who have lived where the Bible is respected, if not carefully studied. "I knew I was not a Christian all the time. I even knew I must be born again, but I just didn't know how. Already when I was eighteen, I was seeking. I wanted to be happy like one of my girl friends who was always so happy.

"My father planned for me to marry a young man I didn't like at all. That was the way they did it in the old country. To get away from him I came to America. But here I was terribly lonesome. I had always been a good girl, but I went too far with men on account of my loneliness when I came to this country. I was afraid to be alone, and wanted someone to care for me and love me.

"Some time before the Billy Graham Crusade, a strange thing happened. My brother, who still is in Germany, had read *Peace with God* in German, and through reading it he had been saved. He sent the book to me, and I read it. I didn't do anything about it then, but a little later my sister asked me to go with her to the meeting. She too had come to America, but she had made her decision while living in Germany. I was glad to go with her, and I have been so thankful since then that she asked me. I received Christ and He accepted me the first night.

"I cannot forget that night. As Billy preached, I cried. I knew in my heart that this was the right thing to do. I remember he said, 'Just believe it now,' and it all seemed so simple, too simple to save anyone. He talked about the witness of the Spirit, and I hadn't the faintest idea what that meant. Now I understand what he meant because it's just the way it says it in the Bible. Everything is just as the Bible tells, and I can't disbelieve it now.

"As Billy finally gave the invitation, I thought he should ask some hard thing for us to do. I just couldn't think that salvation was a gift. I remember I spoke to my sister and asked her if all I had to do was to go forward. She said it was; it's so simple. The preaching of the Bible had been so honest that I couldn't refuse. It was what I had always wanted, so I went forward. A wonderful lady helped me when I came to the counseling room, but I was too pre-occupied to pay much attention to her. She must have thought I wasn't listening. But as I looked at the verses she showed me, I remembered my whole life, and knew I needed forgiveness for many sins. I wept when I thought how much Christ loved me to die for me, and I still can weep when I think of it. I cannot understand how He should have cared for me, but I know He did. It's just like the Bible says. I was so relieved and happy when I had finally come to Christ and He had accepted me.

"I didn't have the slightest idea where to go to church after my decision. I went often to the meetings, but when they were over I knew I wanted to come to know some other believers. I tried three churches. At the first one I went to, the preacher announced a church dance the following week. I knew then I didn't want to go there, for I had come to find someone to pray with and a place to study the Bible. Finally I learned of a church near my home where they had prayer meetings and Bible study during the week as well as preaching from the Bible on Sunday. I have been very happy in that church where so many people believe the Bible and love Christ.

"A big difference has come in our home too. My husband didn't get saved. In fact he doesn't like Mr. Graham's sermons at all. He says that his Gospel is too simple, and he likes something more intellectual. At first, when I told him of my decision, he was angry. He still says mean things about my faith and Billy Graham, but I believe he will come to Christ some time. You see, I don't believe I was a really good wife. I kept insisting that we needed to build a new home where our baby could grow up in fresh air and sunshine. I told him this apartment was no place to live. Now I don't care because I don't feel that it is anything too important. Another thing that I had done was to get someone to watch the baby while I went to the movies. I guess they are all right but I was going almost every day and neglecting my baby and housework. It was costing a lot of money too.

"There are some things about my conversion that I know my husband likes. I never could save any money before. Now I have money left over at the end of the week, and my husband can't understand it. There are so many things in life that are changed when you come to Christ. God has blessed me more than I can ever tell. I remember the years I was looking for this joy and was so unhappy. I wish I had known it all before. I am so busy now with Bible study and fellowship with people who love Christ. Many in our church were converted during the Crusade, and we talk about so many things as we remember the time we came to the Saviour. Our testimony meetings are so wonderful because, even though we all have problems, and some have more now than before, yet the Lord is filling our lives with a joy we didn't think was possible. It's so wonderful that a housewife like me, with a little baby to bring up, can have salvation and can find happiness in the ordinary things that we have to do every day, like washing dishes, dusting, taking care of the baby, and a thousand things I hated before. A verse I like so much is where Jesus said, 'I am come that they might have life, and that they might have it more abundantly.' I thank God I have finally found what I have been searching for, and that He does give the peace and joy He promises."

13. Experiencing Conversion

STUART HAMBLEN has written, "It is no secret what God can do; what He's done for others, He'll do for you." Stuart learned this lesson in the Greater Los Angeles Crusade in the fall of 1949. What God did for Stuart and six thousand others that memorable fall, He has continued to do. It would not be possible to number accurately the entire group that has continued to grow since that time. Those who are familiar with the record know that there are always those whose experiences have never been recorded who attribute their conversion to the Billy Graham Crusades and radio ministry.

Some of them have told their stories with the hope that those who read their testimony will have hope. Many readers will rejoice as they relive their own moment of conversion with each account. Those who have been silent will realize the joy they have forfeited because they have not borne testimony to the grace of God. A few who read will desire the assured knowledge that they have been accepted into the family of God through faith in His Son. It is hoped that those who are strangers to the household of faith will seek the same Lord of whom the converts have given witness.

Conversion is the living experience of the things that are taught in the Bible. Jesus said that the new birth was necessary (John 3:7). Paul said, "If any man be in Christ, he is a new creature . . ." (II Corinthians 5:17). Peter said that the believer is "born again . . . by the word of God, which liveth and abideth for ever" (I Peter 1:23). These are the teachings of the Bible that have become real-life experiences of the sixty thousand converts of the New York Crusade, the fifty-two thousand of the All-Scotland Crusade, the thirty-eight thousand of the London Crusade, or from any of the many other Crusades and Rallies, television and radio programs around the world.

Every person learns most by his own experience. There are some who can learn from the experience of others. Those who have wondered about the converts and their experiences now have the opportunity of learning exactly what happens when a person from the audience responds to the invitation. Not every one is a genuine convert. Some come without the drawing of the Spirit of God. When they do, it is because they have other reasons. Some are just curious. A certain number come to receive some of the blessings of salvation but not the experience of salvation through Christ. There are always the four classifications spoken of by Jesus in Matthew 13. Upon the first group, the Word falls like seed on the wayside and the birds pluck it up. The second group receive the Word with joy but are superficial. A third group hear the Word, but the cares of the world and the deceitfulness of riches choke it out. It is the fourth group that gives such joy for they have depth and become fruitful. From the experience of the converts, learn the lessons they have to teach.

They teach first that few people know what it means to be a Christian. When the converts were asked if they had considered themselves to be Christians, the nearly unanimous answer was "Yes." One young man said "I was almost reared in the church and have always been active in church work. Naturally I assumed that I was a Christian. Another young man said, "I just never thought much about it. I just always thought I was as good as anyone else." A young woman said "I thought I was a Christian because I wasn't a Hindu or Mohammedan." An aged woman said "I thought I was a Christian because I had always been trying to live the best life possible, and I thought God would somehow overlook my mistakes because I had tried."

Every one of the testimonies reveals the ignorance that exists with respect to the Christian faith. Christianity is not primarily a system of ethics, as some have thought. It is not an affiliation with some religious organization as others have thought. Because they did not know what Christianity was, the majority of the converts had just assumed that they were Christians. Their error became obvious as they heard the preaching of the cross of Christ from God's servant Billy Graham.

The second lesson they teach is that they became Christians suddenly, and not by an extended process. Billy Graham frequently says to his audience, "You came into this meeting not thinking that you could leave a new person, but you can be a new person before you go out."

Jesus taught that a man must be born again, and birth is always sudden. There are many preliminary factors, but birth takes place in a moment. Hundreds were converted the first time they attended the Crusade, and for some it was the first time they had attended a religious meeting of any kind. Others were converted after many years of religious instruction, but their conversion came with equal suddenness.

Anyone who has not thought much about the phenomenon of conversion will wonder at the suddenness with which the change takes place. Because they think it is something to be fully understood, they deny the possibility of such dramatic transformations. But conversion can be sudden and it is so because of the possibility of presenting the Gospel in terms of the love of God for the sinner as demonstrated at the cross. When the converts were asked what Scriptural truth had awakened them to their need of the Saviour and their desire to receive Him, they consistently said it was the teaching best expressed in the words, "For God so loved the world, that he gave his only begotten son, that whosoever believeth in him should not perish, but have everlasting life" (John 3:16). This is the verse that Luther called "The little Gospel."

It was enough for them to know that they were the objects of God's infinite love, and that He invited every sinner to come and take of the water of life freely. Once the assurance was clear that their sins had been forgiven, they were then on the way to living a full and vibrant life of faith and challenge.

The experience of the converts has a third lesson to

teach and a truth to illustrate. The Bible says, "If any man
be in Christ, he is a new creature: old things are passed
away; behold, all things are become new." Again and
again they bore witness to the fact that everything was so
new and different. A forgotten man of "skid row," after
being drunk for thirty years, became a sober man in a
moment of time. An addict suddenly lost the craving for
dope. An immoral woman came to one of the Crusade
meetings and went out to live an exemplary life. A discouraged and introspective cripple came to hear the word
and found a supply of grace and love that gave him a new
reason for living and a service he could render to his fellows. A retired school teacher, who had been serving
young people for more than forty years, discovered a new
motive and desire for giving her few remaining years to
witness for Christ. Everyone who receives the Gospel message in an act of believing is that moment made new. A
young man working for a construction company came to
receive Christ. The same night he visited his wife in a
nearby hospital. Instantly she observed the difference. He
was no longer the same proud, selfish husband she had
known. He had suddenly become humble and compassion-
ate. Jesus Christ had come into his poor life to dwell and
he was a new creature. This noticeable change took place
in thousands. Each one became a new creature, just as
the Scripture says (II Corinthians 5:17).

The experiences of the converts also teach us a fourth
lesson. The new birth has no natural explanation. This remarkable transforming crisis in the life of an individual is
best explained in terms of the supernatural. Although the
individual converts may differ from one another in age,

in social class, in educational and intellectual power, in emotional nature and in previous religious training, they all relate their conversion to the Bible. In the preaching, Billy Graham makes no apology for the Bible, but preaches it directly and forcefully. Such directness and forcefulness cannot be forced, but result from a personal confidence in the final authority of the Bible.

The Bible has a central theme. Even though it is a volume containing sixty-six separate books, and though thirty-nine different men were used of God to write its single message, and its time spans more than fifteen centuries, yet it has a remarkable consistency. Its theme, stated in the simplest terms, is the redemption of sinful man through the person and work of Jesus Christ. This is the message that has so effectively and totally changed the lives of thousands. It is no secret formula nor magic employed. It is the time-honored message of the Gospel which is "The power of God unto salvation to every one that believeth . . ." (Romans 1:16).

What makes such sudden and revolutionary changes? It is the miraculous work of the Spirit of God. He is the One who gave the spiritual desire to those who came to seek the Lord. Often He was not recognized, but He was nevertheless working. A beautiful young actress complained of a feeling of desperate emptiness that was so real that she asked her physician to perform an operation. She did not know that the Spirit of God had produced that emptiness that demanded satisfaction. A church-going young man, who had lived a good life, suddenly came to understand certain truth from the Bible that he had never known before, though he had read the same verses many times. He did not know that the Holy Spirit had come to guide men into truth and to give spiritual sight to the blind.

The new birth is miraculous. In an age of humanism and naturalism, it takes place in complete contradiction to the scientific explanation of the human spirit. The same change may take place in the young and the old. The rich and the poor must repent of sin and seek forgiveness through Christ, and as they do so, they both become new. Neither environment nor heredity seem to make a difference.

The fifth lesson that can be learned from the story of the convert is that there is none who is beyond hope. Numbered among the converts were many persons who were socially well-adjusted. They had lived well and achieved success. They had taken advantage of the finer things of life. But there were also those who were the social outcasts. Personal and social immorality had dragged them to the lowest depths until they had lost hope. Alcohol and dope had ruined their lives and there seemed to be no way out.

Jesus had said "I am not come to call the righteous, but sinners to repentance." Many of the hopeless ones who came to the Crusades heard a message that generated hope within them from the very beginning. They heard in song and sermon of the matchless grace of Jesus. They were told of One who suffered cruel torture on a cross to make a way for every man. As they listened they were overwhelmed by the sense of God's love for the destitute.

Those who had lost hope were suddenly awakened to the fact that they were loved. Many of them had come to the place where they thought that no one cared. One attractive girl, when in the depths of drunkenness and immorality, said that she would sometime think of God, but then she would reason, "Why should God be interested in me?" After many months of such desperation she came to a Crusade meeting. There she heard the message of God's love for the unloved. She recalled a Scripture which says "But God commendeth his love toward us, in that, while we were yet sinners, Christ died for us" (Romans 5:8).

The greatest need of the human soul is to be loved. Even the social outcast and fallen woman are capable of responding to a sincere expression of love. In fact, they cannot be expected to respond to any other power. Rejected by society and forgotten by former friends, they are unable to face reality or to trust anyone. There is no hope for them unless they can be convinced that there is someone who loves them.

Messages preached at the Billy Graham Crusades may be sometimes concerned with the contemporary world situation, with the final day of judgment of sinners, with problems of the home and family, or any of the evils of our times. But the emphasis on the love of God for the outcast and the sinner is never absent. That love is fully demonstrated in the cross of Christ (Titus 2:11).

Jesus once said, "And I, if I be lifted up from the earth, will draw all men unto me" (John 12:32). This explains the attraction of the crucified One. There is an attraction as well as an offense in preaching the cross. The self-righteous are offended because they lose their grounds for boasting when they must recognize that salvation is not

by works. By the same message the hopeless and helpless
are encouraged when they realize that there is no sin
greater than God's grace. They are encouraged to hope in
Christ when every other cause for hope is gone.

The final message and truth that is illustrated in the conversion accounts is that the Gospel is still the power of
God for salvation to "every one that believeth" (Romans
1:16). This is the first-century Gospel as preached by the
apostles. In response to the commission of the Saviour,
they went out into all the world to preach. Before long
they had earned the reputation of turning the world up-
side down (Acts 17:6). The armies of the Caesars were
not able to withstand the offensive of the preachers of the
Cross, for what they could never accomplish by force,
the Gospel could accomplish by love.

Napoleon once commented, "Alexander the great,
Caesar and I have founded great empires upon force.
Today our empires are crumbled. Jesus Christ founded a
kingdom based upon love, and today there are millions
that would die for him." This modern-day miracle of conversion to Jesus Christ confirms the faith and hope of
believers everywhere. The Gospel contradicts the world
and is in opposition to it. Yet its attraction is felt in every
generation by men and women of every race. Its attraction is in no way diminished by the technological and
cultural advance of our generation, but is far more perti-
nent to the problems of the day than the method of
modern man. Augustine, the fifth-century leader of Chris-
tion thought, said, "Thou hast formed us for Thyself, and
our soul is restless until it rests in Thee."